The Inspired Life

God's Dream for Your Future

David Cannistraci

and

Chris Cobb

GateWay City Church Publishing
San Jose, California

The Inspired Life:
God's Dream for Your Future
© 2015 by David Cannistraci & Chris Cobb

All Rights Reserved

This book is protected under copyright law of the United States of America. The total or partial reproduction of this book for commercial gain or profit is forbidden. The use of short quotations or occasional page copying for personal or group study is permitted and encouraged.

All Scripture quotations are from the New King James Version. Copyright © 1979, 1980, 1982 by Thomas Nelson, Inc. Used by permission. All rights reserved.

ISBN – 978-0-692-58524-5

Published by

GateWay City Church Publishing
5883 Eden Park Place, San Jose, CA 95138

Acknowledgements

We would like to thank and show our appreciation to the GateWay Publishing editorial team. A big shout out to Karen Greenwell and Carol Cobb for their editing and proofing, Cari Stewart and Jordan Cannistraci for you insight and suggestions, and Shaun Middlebusher for the cover design of this book.

We would also like to thank our patient, loving wives, Kathy and Carol, for steadfastly standing with us during the many hours of writing, praying, editing and then praying some more.

Dedication

This book is dedicated to the members of GateWay City Church. Our vision as a church is *"Inspiring Transformed Lives"*. This is what we live to do and want to impart to our city. We are world changers, and together we attempt to live what this book is all about - the inspired life.

We also dedicate this book to GateWay's founding pastor Apostle Emanuele Cannistraci, affectionately known as Apostle C. You are an example to all of what it means to live the inspired life. Your influence, leadership and love will carry us all for generations to come.

Lastly, we dedicate this work to the people of the San Francisco Bay Area. Our prayer is that all come to know Him, who is the answer for everything. You too can experience an inspired life in Jesus Christ. We are here for you!

Contents

Foreword by Apostle Emanuele Cannistraci	1
A Prophetic Vision – Around a Bonfire	3
Introduction	5
Chapter 1: Welcome to Your Inspired Life: Knowing Jesus Christ	7
Chapter 2: Jesus Christ: Your Blueprint for an Inspired Life	31
Chapter 3: "Follow Me": Answering Your Call to Follow the Master	49
Chapter 4: Relationships: The Power and Purpose of Living Connected	69
Chapter 5: "Shining in the Darkness": The Power of Your Influence	95
Chapter 6: God's Rewards for You!	119

Foreword

There are three trillion stars in the heavens and our God has named them all! In the same way God knows every person who has ever lived. He knows us by name, and He knows every intimate detail about our lives. He created each of us to fulfill a purpose. He established our destiny from the foundation of the world. Now the invitation has gone forth from the courts of heaven for every person to come and experience His wonderful plan for their lives.

This book, *The Inspired Life*, will give you an understanding of God's will for your life. You will discover, within these pages, that God has a plan and His plan includes you. Pastors David Cannistraci and Chris Cobb have laid out for you, the reader, the steps God has taken to draw you to Himself and to unfold this incredible journey in your life. You will discover the life of Jesus Christ, the One who has gone before us and provides the example of what an inspired life is. It is in your relationship with Jesus Christ that you will learn how to live this abundant life.

After reading this book I'm convinced that it will help those new to a relationship with Jesus Christ, as well as seasoned leaders across the body of Christ. This book will help pastors and church leaders make plain where God is taking His people in the future, as He builds His church. The message of the day is to finish His work - and His work is making disciples. My deepest desire and prayer today is for leaders and all believers to capture the essence of what an inspired life is all about; discovering your purpose in fulfilling His. He builds the church, we make disciples; it's that simple. When you step into His purpose you will truly find this Christian walk is the most exciting and fulfilling endeavor you'll ever experience.

I salute the writers of this book and urge church members and leaders everywhere to read and put into practice the principles found in this book.

Apostle Emanuel Cannistraci
November 2015

A Prophetic Vision – Around a Bonfire

As we worshipped together one Sunday morning in August of 2015, the Lord showed Pastor David Cannistraci a powerful vision. His eyes were closed, but he saw it with the eyes of his heart: hundreds of believers gathered around a huge bonfire. He describes, "We were on a beach, and it was cold and dark everywhere. For miles around us, the power grid was down and society languished in the darkness and chill. Yet for those who were gathered there was light, warmth and community. We were confident, lifting our hands in joyful worship. People were connecting, and others were joining us around the fire. There was room for everyone."

The Holy Spirit whispered to him: "In these last days, many will suffer and feel lost in the cold and dark. But my people will gather in clusters. They will stand in the light. They will rejoice because they are safe and connected."

"I thought deeply about our small groups," he later wrote. "I thought of our men's and women's gatherings. I thought about our college services and our youth ministries. I knew we would never neglect the power of community, connection and the GATHER GROW GO strategy which the Lord has given us."

As you pick up this book, understand one thing: We have developed this to strengthen you within a community of faith. Get a copy of the study guide and get involved in a small group. You cannot face the days that are ahead all by yourself. You need a warm circle of friends. And you will find it in the community of those who, like you, are following Jesus and pursuing an Inspired Life.

Introduction

You have been called to live an inspired life! A life filled with God's purpose and plan. A life defined by His destiny and dream for you. A life experiencing the fullness of His presence, power and promise on a continuous basis. Is this life possible? Is it conceivable for you to discover the life God has ordained for you to live? Yes it is, and that is what this book is all about.

Living the inspired life lifts you out of the normal everyday affairs of mankind and into the fulfillment of God's dream for your life. The inspired life God has reserved for you is a life complete with meaning and contentment. It is a life of accomplishment and triumph. And further, it is God's inspired life, lived in and through you that will leave a legacy for years to come.

"The Inspired Life: God's Dream for Your Future" will take you on a journey to not only discover God's dream for you, but also how to step into His destiny to be lived out through you. As you read through the pages you will quickly learn that Jesus Christ, God's Son, is central to living the inspired life. He is our example, our template and the blueprint for the inspired life. And it is through knowing Him personally that His inspired life in imparted to us. As He fills us and matures us as disciples we then begin to live as He did; inspiring this world for the Kingdom of God.

The goal of this short book is to saturate the reader with the potential of God's anointing living in you to inspire others. You too can live out a life that shares the light and love of Jesus Christ to a world in pain, looking for answers. You too can inspire others as Jesus Christ inspired. So as you read through the pages to follow, prayerfully consider God's specific plan for your life. And this plan starts with knowing Jesus Christ, being conformed to His life and culminates in you living a life for Christ.

Come, join us as we open God's word, the Bible and discover a life God had planned for you before time began. It is truly the most amazing, powerful and fulfilling life you will ever experience. It is truly *"The Inspired Life; God's Dream for Your Future"*.

David Cannistraci
Chris Cobb
July, 2015

Chapter 1

Welcome to Your Inspired Life: Knowing Jesus Christ

What if? What if there was a life you could live which exceeded your wildest dreams and imaginations? What if you, today, were presented with an opportunity to live a fulfilled life, a meaningful life, a blessed life, and even a rewarded life? What if the door opened for you to live a life which could lift you above the daily grind and pressures of work, family, and society? A life that is not limited by Wall Street or political agendas? A life beyond the fantasies of Hollywood or the odds of winning the lottery?

We're talking about a life defined by purpose and motivated by destiny. A life stirred with a passion to live and the vision to experience the impossible. What would you do to obtain such a life? How would you respond if presented with this life? Stop and think for a few minutes about the kind of life you'd like to live. Would it be a life with no limits, no barriers, and no humanly set boundaries? Is this type of life available, realistic, and even possible?

The answer to the above question is, yes! Such a life is available to you: a God ordained life. A life which God creates to empower you and which you can experience on a daily basis. A life which was in the mind of God, for you, before time began. A life filled with purpose. A life of answered prayers, Heaven's resources at your disposal, and the power of God available for whatever need you may have in life. This was, and is, God's original plan, to give you a life full of His grace, His love, His power, and His destiny. We call this living the inspired life.

> *Inspire means to "to fill someone with the urge or the ability to do something great."[1]*

What does it mean to inspire? "Inspire" comes from the word "spirit" because it is a picture of inhaling or filling our inner person with breath: "to fill someone with the urge or the ability to do something great." It also means to "stimulate, motivate, affect, influence, move, stir, ignite, trigger, energize, and awaken." We should do that!

This is what this book is all about: how you can step into God's inspired life. It is truly an amazing, exciting, and satisfying life. This is a life based on a relationship with Jesus Christ. How to grow in your relationship with Him. And how to live as He lived. So the more you know Him, the more you will experience what an inspired life is all about.

It this the life you desire and long for? So now you ask, "Where do I start; where can I sign up for such a life?"

It All Begins With Knowing Jesus Christ

> This is the real and eternal life: that they know you, the one and only true God… John 17:3 (MSG)

Everything in creation points to Jesus Christ. He created all

---

[1] Oxford Dictionaries, Oxford University Press, June 29, 2015 <http://www.oxforddictionaries.com/us/definition/american_english/inspire>

[2] Cooperstowners In Canada, "The Greatest Man that Babe Ruth Ever

things and all things are sustained by Him (Colossians 1:17). He is the centerpiece of creation. Jesus Christ is the greatest and most unique person to ever have graced this earth. It was through Jesus Christ that God walked again on this earth as He did in the days of Adam and Eve. And it is still He who walks among us by His Spirit drawing us into a relationship with Him so that He can impart to us His abundant life.

The inspired life is a life of simply knowing Jesus Christ.

You see friends, the inspired life is a life of simply knowing Jesus Christ. But this is so much more than going to church and the rituals of religion. This inspired life is the result of personally and vitally knowing the person of Jesus Christ. He wants to know you, love you, speak to you, and become an integral part of your life. He wants you to know His voice, His heart, and His power in your life. He wants to share and impart to you His wisdom, His purpose, and His plan for you. It is Jesus Christ, the One who is eternally steadfast, omnipotent, sitting on a throne, who desires to come along side you, walk with you, and guide you into His perfect plan. But many would ask what does it really mean to know Jesus Christ? How can I know if I really know Him?

Knowing Jesus Christ is Personal

There is a difference between knowing *about* God and knowing God. We can go to church, Bible school, read books, listen to CD's, watch DVD's, go to conferences, and still not know God personally. We call this "secondhand Christianity." Jesus described it in Matthew 7:21-23:

Not everyone who says to Me, "Lord, Lord," shall enter the kingdom of heaven, but he who does the will of My Father in heaven. Many will say to Me in that day, "Lord, Lord, have we not prophesied in Your name, cast out demons in Your name, and done many wonders in Your name?" And then I will declare to them, "I never knew you; depart from Me, you who practice lawlessness!"

Knowing Jesus Christ is a personal relationship based on firsthand knowledge. If we say, "I know cars," I mean I know about cars, engines, manufacturers, and so on. But if we say, "I know *my* car," I mean I know what my car drives like, where its dings are, and how it handles because I have experienced it. We must know God personally, with firsthand knowledge and faith if we are to be strong in Him and live an inspired life.

If we are going to know God, we must believe that He is a person, not a cosmic force or a higher power. He is a living, thinking, feeling person. He asks questions and gives answers. He visits people. He reveals Himself to us. He deals with us when we sin, blesses us when we obey, comforts us when we mourn, and strengthens us when we wait on Him. He is personal and He can be known.

Knowing Jesus Christ is Experiential

Oh, taste and see that the LORD is good; blessed is the man who trusts in Him! Psalms 34:8

David once went to a restaurant and almost left because of its appearance. "I didn't know if the food would be good but when I tasted it, I knew it was good"! You cannot know something without tasting it or trying it. In the same way, if we've never experienced God, we can't know Him. A relationship with God is something to experience personally. You can feel His love, His peace, sense His presence, and know His joy through His word, in worship, in prayer, and in fellowship with other believers.

Knowing Jesus Christ is Spiritual

> God is Spirit, and those who worship Him must worship in spirit and truth. John 4:24

A lot of people confuse religion with a spiritual relationship with God. Religion is natural, but a relationship with God is spiritual. Church, classes, being discipled, and going to seminars are natural things. They can be helpful, but they are not a substitute for knowing Him in deeper dimensions. When we worship, pray, and fellowship, we are going deeper with God.

You say, "I've been serving the Lord for years! I go to church, read my Bible, and I know the hymns." Yes, but do you know Him as you ought to know Him? The disciples walked with Jesus, ate with Him, and listened to Him for three years, but did not know Him spiritually:

> Thomas said to him, "Lord, we don't know where you are going, so how can we know the way?" Jesus answered, "I am the way and the truth and the life. No one comes to the Father except through me. If you really knew me, you would know my Father as well. From now on, you do know him and have seen him." Philip said, "Lord, show us the Father and that will be enough for us." Jesus answered: "Don't you know me, Philip, even after I have been among you such a long time? Anyone who has seen me has seen the Father." John 14:5-9a

This shows us that the only way to know God is through Jesus Christ. Jesus makes the Father manifest. If you see Him, you see God the Father. Jesus is the way to have a relationship with God. Just two verses after these words, Jesus describes the exploits that follow those who know Him:

> Most assuredly, I say to you, he who believes in Me, the works that I do he will do also; and greater works than these he will do, because I go to My Father. And whatever you ask in My name, that I will do, that the Father may be glorified in the Son. If you ask anything in My name, I will do it. John 14:12-14

Knowing Jesus Christ is ZOE Life

The Bible speaks of God's life and refers to it in the original Greek language as the *zoe* type of life. *Zoe* is a term which defines the type of life found in knowing Jesus Christ. In fact, the phrase "eternal life" in our foundational scripture is translated from *zoe*, which describes the God kind of life:

> "This is real and eternal life (*zoe*)"... John 17:3

Jesus made the above statement while sitting at the Last Supper with His men. He was describing to them the type of life He was about to make available to them. He said, "this is eternal life," and then shared that He was the source, the sustainer, and the empowerment of the life available as a result of knowing Him. Many have thought the phrase "eternal life" speaks of a life off into the future reserved for those entering their eternal state after death. Oh, but friends, Jesus is speaking of life for you here and now. He didn't qualify this life for you after you die. No,

Jesus was describing the *zoe* life which is available to you today.

The inspired life is the *zoe* type of life. It is the God life. It is the life empowered by the Holy Spirit, refreshed by His presence, carried by His love, and lived out day by day as He leads and guides. The original meaning of *zoe* speaks of the kind of life Jesus lived while on this earth. Jesus personified the *zoe* type of life. He was our example. He demonstrated a life of absolute fullness resulting from His Father living in Him by the Holy Spirit.

If you want to see an example of the inspired life, then look at Jesus Christ.

If you want to see an example of the inspired life, then look at Jesus Christ. Jesus knew no fear and never lost an argument or a challenge. He walked in perfect love, tore down demonic strongholds, and lived above the natural realm as He healed the sick, walked on water, and worked miracles among us. Then He went on to offer us this same type of life as we come to know Him.

The inspired *zoe* life is imparted to you the moment you turn your life over to God and receive Jesus Christ as your Lord and Savior. Or, we can say, the inspired life is implanted in you the moment you believe in Him. Now you have available the quality of life Jesus Christ lived when He walked on this earth. It is God presence living in you. It's His Spirit anointing and empowering you. It is His promises and purpose that come alive and are experienced through you. And all of this results from simply knowing Jesus Christ. This truly is an inspired life—knowing Jesus Christ.

Now we will cover five essential steps God took to create and make available to you His inspired life. Our prayer is that you will grasp the indescribable and unparalleled life available only through knowing Jesus Christ. For it is in knowing Jesus Christ that His very life is shared with you. Are you ready? Let's dive in.

God's Plan to Share His Inspiring Life With You

1. God Had a Dream—and His Dream Included You

God knew what he was doing from the very beginning. Romans 8:29 (MSG)

Nobody was before Him. And there will be nobody after Him. He is God. He has no predecessor. He will have no successor. He stands alone in the solitude of Himself. And while in this eternal state, which we'll never understand or comprehend, God had a dream. He thought of you and I.

He planned out the details of the heavens and the earth. God planned and knew each person to ever walk this earth. He knew our form, our make up, and the number of our days. We're told:

Your eyes saw me before I was put together. And all the days of my life were written in Your book before any of them came to be. Psalms 139:16 (NLV)

Wow! What was God thinking? When did He come up with His plan for you? What is this book that we're told our life was written in before time began? Friends, in our present limited, finite state we will never understand or comprehend what went on in the courts of heaven before time began. The Bible profoundly tells us our God is great, "nor can the number of His years *be* discovered " (Job 36:26).

> *Jesus Christ knew every detail about your life. He looked forward to fellowship with you. He has an inspired life awaiting you.*

God was thinking about you way back before time began. Somewhere, sometime, using human terms, God came up with a dream to make you and He has a desire to love you and be with you. The Bible says God is love (1 John 4:8). Yes, it was God's love dream to form you, create you, and it was His desire to be with you. We're told this was His plan "before the beginning of time" (2 Timothy 1:9).

Imagine with me, for a few moments, how God thought of each and every person who has ever been born. He knew what we were to look like. He knew our thoughts, our actions, and then He wrote down in His book all the details of our lives.

Now, of course, this is an over simplification since there are many questions when this topic is discussed. Such as, if God is good then why all the pain and suffering? Was this a part of God's plan? We obviously won't be able to answer these questions. But we do know that God is love and His dream from the beginning was a good dream and His plan was a good plan.

He knew your form. He knew your days. He knew when you would be born and where you'd live. He knew every detail about your life. He looked forward to knowing you. He has an inspired life awaiting you. But now the question comes up: how was God was going to make this dream into a reality?

Given that He also knew mankind was going to fall into sin and experience the resulting suffering and pain, how was God going to dream, foresee man's fall, and then cause His desire to still be fulfilled? Ah, here's the good news: it's called the gospel of Jesus Christ.

2. Let the Transformation Begin

He chose them to become like his Son. Rom. 8:29 (NTL)

God made a decision. His decision involved sending His Son to Earth for a variety of specific reasons, one of which was to give us an example of how to live a truly inspired life. Yes, Jesus Christ's life; lived in obscurity as a humble carpenter, was an example of what an inspired life can actually be. Whole books and volumes have been written describing in great detail who this God-Man was and what He accomplished. Libraries and web pages are full of the far reaching influence He has had upon mankind.

Included in this decision was God's plan for His people to become like His Son. We're told in scripture that we are called to be "conformed" to His image (Romans 8:29). This speaks of us "having the same form as one another, and being similar to" God's Son. In other words a major focus of God's plan was for Jesus Christ to be Heaven's blueprint and for us to be molded and formed into the likeness of Him.

George "Babe" Ruth

The legendary home run king, Babe Ruth, was asked who he credited his success to as a major league baseball player. Without hesitating the Babe said it was Brother Mathias. Babe was raised in a Catholic School and home. It was Brother Mathias who took the young George Ruth and taught him how to pitch and hit spending hours each day with the young man who would go on to set many records. It was Brother Mathias who "molded" the Babe into the image of what he was to become.[2]

Read through the four gospels of Matthew, Mark, Luke, and John and take a close look at Jesus' life. Then step back and realize you just saw an example of what God wants you to become like. Yes, God's plan is to work in you and through you so you, too, can experience life as Jesus lived it. God's plan is to transform your life to live, think, walk, act, and overcome like Jesus Christ. The Bible says, "As He is so are we in this world" (1 John 4:14). In other words, His life is what our life is to become. Consider that Jesus Christ:

>Knew no fear
>Had no barriers
>Didn't know limitations
>Never knew defeat
>Never experienced lack
>Didn't give in to weakness
>Lived above sin
>Didn't allow men to define Him
>Was never confused
>Never gave in to temptations
>Didn't wring His hands out of worry
>Knew where He came from
>Knew where He was going
>Knew His Father was with Him at all times

---

[2] Cooperstowners In Canada, "The Greatest Man that Babe Ruth Ever Knew was a Canadian, July, 2010,
http://cooperstownersincanada.com/2010/07/17/the-greatest-man-that-babe-ruth-ever-knew-was-a-canadian/

> Pleased the Father in all things
> And many more . . .

There it is friends, a blueprint and a pattern of living the Father desires to make a reality in your life. The Bible tells us:

> He decided from the outset to shape the lives of those who love him along the same lines as the life of his Son… Romans 8:29 (MSG)

So, what you see when you look at Christ's life is a reflection of what God intended for you to become. Do you desire to live an inspired life? Then look at Jesus' life. His perfect, sinless, and victorious life is available to you as you come to know Him. He wants to share His life with you. In fact, He wants to live in you and give you the same power to live that He had. Chapter 2 of this book will go into greater detail of the life and ministry of Jesus Christ. There is much to learn about our Lord and His role model for us. How does God begin to step into our lives and start the transformation into the inspired life? Read on.

3. God is Calling!

> After God made that decision of what his children should be like, he followed it up by calling people by name; Romans 8:30 (MSG)

It was a sad day on earth. The Father's heart was broken. For, you see, God's prize creation, Adam, had fallen. God created the heavens, the earth, and the animals, and set His man and woman in the garden for the express purpose of having someone to love and enjoy life with. But something very tragic took place. Adam and Eve sinned. Fellowship was broken. There was a breach in Father God's relationship with His creation. We're told God went looking for His man:

> The LORD God called unto Adam, and said unto him, "**Where are you?**" Genesis 3:9

God called but no one answered. Adam was hiding in shame and fear. Now Adam was probably twenty to forty feet away hiding in the bushes as the Lord was looking for Him. And God made a decision right then, on the spot, to draw His creation, mankind, back to Him. It was many, many years before Jesus Christ came and created a way for mankind to walk those twenty to forty feet back into God's presence without the shame, guilt, and regret of sin.

Down through the years God began calling out to men and women. There were those who heard His call and began to respond. God called to Noah. He spoke with Abraham. He appeared to Moses and Joshua. He woke up Samuel in the night. He spoke through prophets. He appeared in dreams and visions to men and women. Yes, God was taking the initiative. God was on a mission! He was calling! He had a plan and the plan included that mankind would again hear His voice.

The day came when God Himself stepped into this earth again in the form of His Son, Jesus Christ. And the same person who called out to Adam, many years beforehand, came walking along the shores of Galilee looking for people He could again call out to. Yes, the day came when mankind heard the words for the very first time:

> "Follow me.... " Mark 1:17

And that call to "follow me" has been going forth for several thousand years and will continue as Jesus Christ is calling out to all people everywhere, in every nation, and in every tongue.

Can You Hear Him?

For God saved us and called us… 2 Tim. 1:9a

God is calling. Can you hear Him? He's calling out to you, but can you discern His voice? If you get real quiet and spend time turning your ear toward Heaven you are promised to hear the voice of His call. Jesus said, "my sheep hear my voice" (John 10:27). Jesus says that when the Holy Spirit comes He will speak and share with you things to come (John 16:13). Is God speaking and calling out to you? Absolutely!

God is calling. Can you hear Him?

The first call God makes to you is the call to draw you to Himself in order for you to come to know Him. Your response when you hear the call is to receive Him as your Lord, allow Him to forgive you as you confess your sin, and usher you into a new life in Him. This call is the call of salvation. And today, if you've never fully and totally responded to His call, then we encourage you to do so. God is calling. Are you going to answer Him? Do so today.

God's Been Calling You From Birth

The Bible shows God has been calling out to you even when

you were formed in your mothers womb. And God's call has continued to follow you throughout your life. For example, here is a short list of men called by God from their mother's wombs:

Isaac	Genesis 21
Jacob	Genesis 25
Moses	Exodus 2
Samuel	1 Samuel 3
David	Psalms 139
Israel, as a people	Isaiah 44:2
Jeremiah	Jeremiah 1
John the Baptist	Luke 1
Jesus	Luke 1
Paul the Apostle	Galatians 1

What does this mean to you, the reader? Well, from this you can learn and trust that you, too, were called from eternity past, formed in your mother's womb, and are today being drawn to Him as He calls out to you.

Why God has gone to such extent and effort to reach to you? Simple, He wants you to know Him. He wants you to experience eternal life, the *zoe* type of life. Yes, His inspired life. Read through the Bible and you'll find God is relentless in pursuit of you. David said, "Where can I go from your presence…" (Psalms 139:7). He couldn't escape it. God's love and Spirit will track you down and in patience consistently knock on the door of your heart. John said of Jesus, "I stand at the door. I knock. If you hear me call and open the door, I'll come right in… " (Rev. 3:20, MSG).

But is this call to you without a price? No, there was a price paid for you, and all of mankind, to be drawn back to know Him. What was this price? Read on . . .

4. The Price Was Paid for His Inspired Life

Those he called, he put right with himself; Romans 8:30 (GNT).

It's been called the Gospel of Jesus Christ. Some refer to it as God's good news. To others it's known as God's plan of salvation. Simply stated, it is the price He paid to make a way for you to return to Him.

After Adam and Eve sinned, the human race was cast into spiritual darkness and was, from that point, destined to be eternally separated from God. We need to completely grasp this truth, because without it we'll never <u>know</u> and fully understand why a price had to be paid to redeem us and purchase us back to God. Mankind was lost. Sin had sentenced us to a life under the dominion of darkness and to forever know nothing but pain, sorrow, bondage, and guilt.

The justice of God demands that there be repercussions for sin. The Bible says, "the soul that sins shall die" (Ezekiel 18:20). We're also told in God's word that the "wages of sin is death…" (Romans 6:23).

Thus, you needed to pay the price for your sin. But the good news, yes, the greatest news ever, to unfold for mankind is that God decided before time began that He would send His Son to pay the price of sin. Jesus was to be your substitute. The Father God placed His wrath, judgment, and punishment for your sin on His Son. It was Jesus' sacrifice on the cross and the shedding of His blood that met the demands of God's justice.

It was Jesus' death for you that frees you from sin. It is His blood that was offered that cleanses you from sin. And the stipulation was, and still is, that if you would believe and receive Jesus Christ as your substitute, then, and only then, would God declare you right, clean, forgiven, and able to stand before Him again. Thus we have the term "salvation." Yes, you can now be rescued from a life eternally separated from God and from unending darkness.

The Bible says, "whoever shall call upon the Lord shall be saved" (Romans 10:13). The result of this salvation presents us back to the Father God in a right standing position. This is referred to as being righteous before God. The Bible tells us that if anyone believes in Christ that the "old things have passed away..." (2 Corinthians 5:17). That is, the old life, the old ways of living, and the old bondages are gone. We now have available the opportunity to be the very righteousness of Christ before God (2 Corinthians 5:21).This means you can stand before God free from any sense of shame, guilt, sorrow, and sin. This is truly good news!

God now moves you from a life of bondage and darkness and ushers you into His Kingdom's rule and reign.

But it gets better! Not only are you saved and forgiven, you also have a change of address. God now moves you from a life of bondage and darkness and ushers you into His Kingdom's rule and reign. What does this mean to you?

Let's explain it this way. Before you knew God, you lived under the authority of darkness and the "prince of the power of the air" (Ephesians 2:2). When a person is born again, not only are they cleansed by the redeeming blood of Jesus Christ, they are also pulled out of darkness and translated into God's Kingdom. It's like stepping onto the transporter in Star Trek and beaming out of one placed and into another. The Bible puts it this way:

> For he has rescued us from the kingdom of darkness and transferred us into the Kingdom of his dear Son. Colossians 1:13 (ESV)

It is this "transference" that ushers you into a life of knowing Jesus Christ. You are transferred from darkness and into His Kingdom. You are delivered, rescued, and presented into a place where the inspired life is now available to you.

Oh friends, our prayer is that you can grasp the power and potential of this salvation. The price paid is so complete that you're told your sins are thrown into the depths of the sea (Micah 7:19). God says, "I'll no longer remember your sins…" (Hebrews 8:12). And now you can stand before God, free from the power of sin over your life, and can enter into the abundant life, the *zoe* life, the inspired life Jesus Christ. This is the life Jesus was speaking of when He said in John 10:10:

> My purpose is to give them a rich and satisfying life. (NLT)

> I have come that they may have life, and have it to the full. (NIV)

> I came so they can have real and eternal life, more and better life than they ever dreamed of. (MSG).

This, our friends, is the basis of living an inspired life. God planned it before time began and made a way for us to be ushered into a life He had planned for us all along. And better yet, not only does this life free us from bondage and sin, it also introduces us into a place of knowing Jesus Christ and the sharing of His eternal glory.

5. God's Rewards for You

Let's start this section off by stating clearly that only God is to be worshipped and the He alone is to receive glory, honor, and praise. There is one God and He will not allow anyone or anything to take His rightful place. Jesus Himself said, "'You must worship the LORD your God and serve only him" (Luke 4:8).

That said, there is also a theme throughout the Bible where we get a glimpse of God not only rescuing us from darkness and welcoming us into His Kingdom, but we also see where the eternal God, who lives in matchless glory, desires to share, recognize, award, and honor His people before all creation. Yes, there is in the heart of God to share of Himself with His people, His family, and those He has redeemed. The Bible says:

> Those he called, he also made right with him; and those he made right, he also glorified. Romans 8:30

The phrase "glorified" here speaks of God himself desiring to "make renowned, to bestow dignity and worth upon someone."[3] It also refers to God openly acknowledging, honoring, and celebrating someone. Jesus said:

> The Father will honor anyone who serves me. John 12:26

We have an example of the Father honoring His Son when He said, "This is my beloved Son in whom I am well pleased" (Matthew 3:17). It was the Father who recognized and celebrated His Son. And, in like manner, the Father will honor those that are

---

[3] Blueletter Bible, Quoting Strong Concordance, G1392, <http://www.blueletterbible.org/lang/lexicon/lexicon.cfm?Strongs=G13

His.

Another example is seen in the return of the prodigal son (Luke 15:11-32). The father lavished his love on the lost son and then placed him in a place of honor within the family. The son, upon his return, was simply looking for food and a place to live. But, oh, the father wanted to quickly erase any reflection of the tragic past of the son and put him back into a place of honor and celebration. We are told that the father said:

> "We're going to feast! We're going to have a wonderful time! My son is here—given up for dead and now alive! Given up for lost and now found!" And they began to have a wonderful time. Luke 15:24 (MSG).

What does this mean for you? These scriptural truths show God not only loves you, wants you to know His Son, but that there is also a time of honoring and celebrating your return to Him. The Bible says:

> There is joy in the presence of the angels of God over one sinner who repents. Luke 15:10

If you are born again into His Kingdom, then you qualify for God's blessing and honor. Jesus explains it this way:

> The glory which You gave Me I have given them, that they may be one just as We are one. John 17:22

Jesus Christ desires to share the honor of His Father with us. He wants to bestow upon us the same blessing that the Father gave to Him. And the result of this sharing is that we, too, will be one with Him as He is one with the Father. Friends, this is the inspired life; a life that knows Jesus, receives His honor and blessing, and a life that elevates us into a place where we are celebrated before all creation.

Jesus Christ desires to share the honor of His Father with us.

The writer of the letter to the Hebrews speaks of God's creation as being "crowned with glory and with honor" (Hebrews 2:7). Here again the Father is looking to bestow upon His people, which includes you, a crown that identifies you as one of His. And throughout eternity God's people will share in God's glory and splendor together with Him, celebrating the Lamb that was slain, the Lord Jesus Christ. And, as the Bible says, there will be times when we will cast our crowns before Him and give Him all honor and praise and glory (Revelation 4:10).

Dr. Tommy Osborn

Years ago the late Tommy Osborn, an evangelist to the nations, was conducting an outdoor service in Africa where thousands came out to hear the gospel. It was at the close of one of the services when a young man was brought up to the stage to meet Dr. Osborn. This young man had been powerfully delivered and saved that night by the power of God. For, before that evening, this young man lived in a trash dump, wore no clothes, and would attack people as they passed by.

As Dr. Osborn preached, the power of God hit the young man and he was delivered and came to his senses. Others saw this, clothed him, and brought him up to the platform. His testimony was shared that night of how

God set this man free and how he was gloriously saved. After the service, Dr. Osborn took the young man and had him bathed, and cleaned up. He bought him a suit and dress shoes and brought him back to the service the next night. As the worship began others saw a clean shaved, handsome young man standing with Dr. Osborn on the platform at this large outdoor gathering. And they were shocked to find out later in the service that this was the very man who the day before was living in a trash dump, naked, and in bondage.

Thus, in one short twenty-four hour period, God took a demonized man out of the trash dumps, cleaned him up, and had him sitting on the platform next to the man of God who was preaching that night. He literally went from the pit, to a place of honor over night!

This is a picture of what happens when we're born again in God's kingdom. We are taken out of darkness and bondage and placed with Jesus in a place of honor and celebration!

In Summary

A truly inspired life is one of knowing Jesus Christ. You have this life available today. You have an opportunity to receive *zoe* life, the life of God flowing in and through your soul. This life was made available through Jesus' death and resurrection. It is given to you when you receive Him into your heart. Today the Holy Spirit is looking for those who are hungry, open, and looking to live an inspired life. If that is your desire, then say this prayer with all your heart and get ready for Heaven to open up and let the celebration begin!

Lord Jesus, thank you for dying for me and offering me a new life. Thank you for forgiving me, and welcoming me into Your Kingdom. This day, Lord, my desire is to know You. Thank you for wanting to know me. Thank you for working in my life to draw me to You. This day I choose to live my life for You. I ask that You fill me with Your Holy Spirit and impart to me the life which only You can give. Thank You for leading, guiding, healing, restoring, and making a way when things seem impossible. This day I worship You, bless You, and thank You for leading me to Your inspired life. In Jesus' name, AMEN!

Chapter 2

Jesus Christ: Your Blueprint for an Inspired Life

Those whom God had already chosen he also set apart to become like his Son, Romans 8:29 (GNT)

No one in the history of mankind has touched more lives, influenced more people, and completely altered history than Jesus Christ. His life, works, words, character, examples, and stories can be found in every nation, country, village, and town. He has impacted, and still is impacting, the intellectual and the lowly, the strongest and the less fortunate.

Jesus Christ is still influencing every sector of life: male and female, young and old, every race, every color of skin, and every religious tradition. Truly, as the Bible says, the world cannot contain all that has been done, accomplished, and impacted by this One, the Carpenter from Galilee (John 21:25).

Even today, Jesus Christ is radically impacting, influencing, and restoring people's lives. Scores of people every day are meeting and being introduced to Him for the first time. Oh friends, Jesus Christ is as active and involved in the affairs of mankind as ever before in history. He has an agenda, a time schedule, and a mission to fulfill. He said, "I will build my church" (Matthew 16:18). And that is exactly what He is doing today throughout the earth. He's building His *"ekklesia"*, His church. He is "gathering people everywhere into His assembly of called ones."4

Do you want to see the perfect example of a truly inspired life? Then look no further than Jesus Christ. He is our blueprint. He is our example. He is the template, the outline, and the fundamental starting point for every person on this earth.

> **Mohammed**
>
> Mohammed, a high ranking imam from Iran was sent to New Zealand to start a new Islamic Mosque. Several months after he arrived, while preparing to retire for the night and go to bed, someone opened the door to his locked apartment room and walked in. Mohammed was stunned and immediately froze in fear and awe when he saw that the individual who entered his room was Jesus Christ in person, flesh and bone. Jesus pointed at Mohammed and then at the Koran, and said, "You don't need that, you need Me!" And then Jesus disappeared. Mohammed instantly began to pray, cry out to God, and received Jesus Christ as His Lord and Savior.

The starting point for us to truly live an inspired life is simply to follow Jesus Christ. Contained within this invitation to follow Him is the opportunity to truly know Him more completely than we will know any other person on this earth. Jesus Christ is inviting us into His life; to walk with Him, think like Him, love like Him, overcome like Him, and experience the power of an endless life like Him. This, our friends, is the opportunity of a

---

[4] Blueletter Bible, quoting Strongs, number G1392
<http://www.blueletterbible.org/lang/lexicon/lexicon.cfm?Strongs=G1392&t=KJV>

lifetime.

Just think, Jesus Christ invites you today to a place with Him where you can hear His voice, learn of His ways, be filled with His courage and boldness, and share in the secrets of creation. It is as you know Him, experience Him, hear from Him, and are filled with Him that you are transformed into His image, His likeness, His character, and His joy. Yes, it is Jesus Christ who desires to step into your life to walk with you and through you in this world. The potential of Jesus living in you is staggering! And it is available to you today!

The purpose of this chapter is to take you on a journey. As you with walk with Jesus Christ over the next few pages, and discover God's plan to transform you and lift you up, you will learn how to live an inspired life like His Son. You are to live like Him!

It is a process. God's plan takes time. There are challenges to overcome, fears to quell, sorrows to heal, and doubts to dispel. But it is worth it all, as the Master takes you on this journey of growth so you, too, can live an inspired life like Him.

As you read through the next few pages allow the Holy Spirit to begin something new in your heart. Allow Him to birth in you the possibility that you can rise up to a new realm of living, a new hope of enduring, and a fresh life of overcoming, as Jesus Christ lives in you and through you to inspire the world again.

It Began With His Father

The water was still soaking through His robe, and His body was still wet from the Jordan River when all of a sudden the Heavens opened and the Father spoke:

This is my beloved Son in whom I am well pleased.
Matthew 3:17

Then it began. The Father had placed His stamp of approval upon His Son. Right after His baptism Jesus went into the wilderness, fasted forty days, confronted Satan, wrestled through His purpose and identity, and came out in the power of the Holy Spirit (Luke 4:14). He then departed northward into Galilee and began His ministry. The world has never been the same since!

The inspired life of Jesus was sustained throughout His ministry by His relationship with His Father.

Jesus' Relationship With His Father

Over sixty times in the gospel of John alone, Jesus refers to His Father. Who Jesus was, and all that He accomplished was in direct relationship to His Father. It was His Father who directed His steps, shared the secrets of Heaven, and empowered Him to do the impossible. It was His Father who He prayed to for guidance, leaned on as He carried His cross, and looked forward to seeing again after His resurrection.

Time and space does not allow us to delve deeply into this Father and Son relationship. But suffice it to say that it is the starting point for our transformation into the image of Christ. We, also, are to come into a relationship with the Father. Jesus said, "the Father himself loves you" (John 16:27). He said, "It is the Father's good pleasure to give you His kingdom" (Luke 12:32). It is the Father who desires to reward and bless you (Matthew

6:4,6,18). And there are many other promises, verses, and blessings we can list all referring to a relationship with Father God. But perhaps the most powerful is the promise of the Father to honor and bestow affirmation, dignity, and worth. Jesus said, "My Father will honor the one who serves me" (John 12:26).

One of the primary reasons it is imperative you understand the Father's relationship with Jesus Christ is because we, for the most part, live in a fatherless generation. That is, there is an increasing number of our population who come from broken homes, shattered families, and/or are born into generations of families where there is no father in the home. There are now scores of books and studies out today which confirm the devastation and impact this has had on our society and culture.

But there is good news: even if there has never been a father figure in your life, the Heavenly Father is as much available and yearning to know you as He did His Son Jesus Christ. Yes, your Father God has a passion for you to know Him in the same measure and way as Jesus Christ.

Your Relationship With the Father

Jesus tells the story of "the prodigal son" in Luke, chapter 15. When the son hit rock bottom he remembered the food and the living conditions of the slaves in his father's house. He thought perhaps there was hope for him to return to his father's home. But, as the story goes, it was his father who saw the son coming back, ran to him, and immediately wanted to correct the devastation and destruction that were the result of the son's decisions. The father ignored the planned speech of repentance and sorrow from the son. The father saw the pain in his son's eyes. He heard the sorrow in his voice. He smelled the filth of the pig pen and he saw the slumping shoulders of a young man defeated and failing in life. The father desperately acted to draw his son into his love. He wanted to rescue him from months, and perhaps years, of waste and disappointment. And it all began with a kiss.

> *The father desperately acted to draw his son into his love. He wanted to rescue him from months, and perhaps years, of waste and disappointment. And it all began with a kiss.*

Did the son make mistakes and live out wrong choices? Sure. Did he rebel, become self-centered, and walk away by his own volition? Absolutely! But nevertheless, the father kissed the son and lavished his love upon him. In so doing, the son quickly felt he was not being judged, condemned, or destined to be an outcast from the family. No, the father sent a message to the son with his kiss that he was glad that his son had come home! He was welcomed! He was loved, accepted, and was to be honored again as one of the family.

> "Quick! Bring the finest robe in the house and put it on him. Get a ring for his finger and sandals for his feet. And kill the calf we have been fattening. We must celebrate with a feast, for this son of mine was dead and has now returned to life. He was lost, but now he is found." So the party began. Luke 15:22-24

Has the Party Begun for You?

Have you been kissed by the Father? There are many believers in the church who have never, ever experienced this love and kindness from our Father. They have never been kissed and embraced by Him. They live a religious life of conditions, rules, requirements, guilt, pressures, and, oh, if they sinned look out, God's wrath is ready to be released!

Friends, we start our transformation into living the inspired life by understanding our life is to be a reflection of Jesus Christ. You, too, are invited into the same lifestyle and relationship with the Father that Jesus had. So the question then is: do you want to live as Jesus Christ did? Do you desire to know Him, experience Him, hear from Him, and walk with Him? Then allow Him to introduce you to His Father. Come, says the Spirit of God, and allow the Father to love you as He loved His Son. Come and He will begin the transformation into a life inspired by the Father.

Jesus Christ: Our Example of an Overcoming Life

Jesus Christ never sinned. Oh, He was tempted. We're told He was tempted in all the same ways as we are (Hebrews 4:15). He was 100% God and 100% Man. He was God manifest in the flesh (1 Timothy 3:16). And as the God-Man, Jesus had to choose, on a daily basis to yield His life, His mind, His will, and His motives to His Father. He came to fulfill the will of His Father. Jesus said, "I have come to do your will" (Hebrews 10:9).

The reason we touch on this topic is because Jesus, as our example of living an inspired life, faced many, and difficult challenges. This is important for us to understand so that we don't paint a false picture of living an inspired life free of difficulties, hardships, and tests along the way. But with Jesus as our example, we will discover His grace to empower us to face head on the daily temptations that seek to derail our lives of victory.

Jesus Learned to Obey Through Difficult Challenges

Jesus Christ, as Man, didn't automatically receive a fully developed disposition and character of obedience. No, Jesus, we are told, needed to learn obedience. What does this mean? For us, it shows that while He was 100% God, Jesus, as 100% man, had to make choices that led to the total obedience to the Father's will. Jesus gives us an example of what it means to make Godly, wise, and even difficult choices that were consistent with the will of His Father. We are told that Jesus:

…learned obedience by the things He suffered. Hebrews 5:8

Here, "learn" tells us that He yielded over His will to the Father day by day and thus created the inner character that correctly made wise choices. But then the above verse shows how Jesus learned obedience. Yes, He learned by the things He suffered, or by the life experiences that came His way, and His choices to continue in the Father's will.

Jesus Committed Himself to Doing His Father's Will

Jesus said, "Behold, I have come to do Your will, O God." Hebrews 10:9

Jesus Christ, as 100% man and 100% God, needed to make a choice with regards to committing and doing the will of His Father. Could He have ignored and walked away from God's will for His life? There was the potential for this because He was 100% man. Since He totally identified with mankind at all points Jesus faced the same dilemma followers of Christ face – choosing to do the will of God. Jesus had to choose to obey and fulfill the will of His Father, even when it meant discomfort, rejection, hardship and pain. There was something inside of Jesus that said, "I have come to do Your will". There was a resolve that said, "Regardless of what I face in life, I must commit to and fulfill the will of God".

Notice as you read through the gospels all the times when Jesus faced adversity and temptation. Satan tried to get Him off track in the 40 day wilderness fast. The religious people of the day tried to get Him off course with threats to kill Him. His own family thought Jesus has lost His mind (Mark 3:21). But there was something stronger working on the inside of Jesus Christ. There was the pull of the Holy Spirit to lead Him into the perfect will of His Father. There was the keeping power of His Father's grace that protected Him and comforted Him. The will of His Father was the priority. Doing His Father's will was not negotiable.

Living the inspired life does have it challenges. We today, as followers of Christ, must also make a choice to do the will of God. Even in hard times we must choose to obey, choose to act and endure the challenge of doing the will of God. There is something inside a disciple of Christ that says, "I too have come to do Your will". It takes commitment, fortitude and resolve. Our priority is to please God in all we do. We need to make it our aim to please Him, obey Him, love Him and fulfill His will in our lives.

Jesus Trusted the Father in Hard Times

Peter gives us insight as to the character and demeanor of Jesus Christ when He was faced with difficult times. We are told that "people insulted Christ, but He did not insult them in return" (1 Peter 2:23). Peter goes on to show us that when challenged, Jesus trusted His Father, the One who judges rightly, to take care of him (1 Peter 2:23b).

Can you let God your Father take care of you? When you are challenged by other people, sometimes very ungodly people, can you do as Jesus did and simply turn the situation over to the Father?

You see, as we are being formed into Christ's image, there is also the work of grace to give us the strength of character and soul to live as Jesus did. And there is the power of His Spirit to live in us and give us the ability to trust the Father with our everyday affairs, even the most difficult ones. As we grow in this grace, we'll discover the inspired life is an overcoming life. Not a life free from criticism, threats, and hardship, but a life that rises above the criticisms, threats, and hardships even as Jesus did. A life that trusts God.

Jesus Endured, Even on the Cross

There was a reason that Jesus Christ had to go through the cross. The cross of Christ was the price to be paid for you to enter into His inspired life. Forgiveness of sin, breaking of the curse, and the gift of eternal life is yours because of His cross. But along the way in Jesus' ministry, He said that we, too, would need to carry our crosses (Matthew 16:24). So, not only did Jesus carry His cross, but you have to decide daily to carry your cross.

> *The cross of Jesus Christ is central to living an inspired life.*

Friends, the cross of Christ is the deciding factor between a life of bondage and freedom, a life of confusion or knowing the will of God. You see, the cross is central to living an inspired life. It is the decision to take up your cross that will lead you to decide to say "no" to a life of bondage and guilt and will usher you into His life of peace and joy. We are told in the Bible what we are to do:

> Look unto Jesus, the author and finisher of our faith, who for the joy that was set before Him endured the cross. Hebrews 12:2

Did you catch that phrase, "who for the joy set before Him"? Jesus saw something beyond the cross and that was the joy of His Father for having fulfilled His purpose on this earth. We, too, endure the pain of our crosses. That is, the slander, the criticism, the temptation to deny, run, and throw in the towel to sin. All believers in Christ will have a cross to carry. And it will show up in a variety of ways. How? Just follow Jesus and look at all He went through and you'll have a picture of what your cross may bring you. Nevertheless, we are encouraged to:

> Lay aside every weight, and the sin which so easily ensnares us, and let us run with endurance the race that is set before us. Hebrews 12:1

The challenge and triumph of transformation is experienced as you learn obedience, trust your Father, and endure your cross. You, too, need to lay aside everything that would hold you back from God's best for your life. You, too, need to decide to run the race set before you. Victory is assured you, as it was to Jesus, if you keep your eyes on the prize, the finish line, and press on into His inspired life!

The Inspired Life—On Assignment

Jesus Christ was here on earth with an assignment. He came for a specific reason, at a pre-determined time in history, and with a very specific agenda He needed to accomplish. As you read through the gospels it becomes very clear that Jesus Christ had a mission to fulfill. He lived His life on purpose. He lived a life foreordained by the Father, prophetically spoken of by men and women years before, and a life destined to leave a legacy for all mankind.

You have a life waiting for you filled with His purpose and His plan. You have a mission to fulfill, a purpose to live out, and a legacy to leave for mankind. But what is your mission, your assignment, and legacy to look like? Well, just look at Jesus Christ and you have a template whereby you are to live out.

Jesus Touched Lives

Jesus Christ came to seek and save the lost. He offered love, lifted the frail, healed the sick, and blessed the multitudes. He forgave sinners and gave strength to the weak. He protected the downcast and defended the feeble. He offered hope, encouraged faith, demonstrated grace, and blessed the little children. He broke the power of darkness, covered the shame of the guilty, and was available for the tempted and lowly. He gave hope, shared a new joy, and told the people that Father God loved them!

Yes, Jesus touched lives. No one ever before or since has impacted lives like Jesus Christ. And now He desires to live through you to continue touching lives. Yes, the inspired life is a life where you live like Jesus and touch other's lives like Jesus did. Just think, all that He came to do was for your example of what you, too, can do as He lives through you. Jesus said:

> Whoever puts his trust in Me can do the things I am doing. He will do even greater things than these because I am going to the Father. John 14:12 (NLV)

You can be a blessing to others. You, with Christ's love in you, can lift up the downcast, offer forgiveness, heal the wounded and sick, and be a reflection of Christ on this earth. Listen friends, you may be the closest likeness of Christ those around you will ever see. You may have family members, loved ones, or co-workers who have never experienced God's love or Jesus' grace.

Yet, could it be that as you are changed more and more into Christ's image, you, too, will begin to live out His mission, His assignment, and His purpose? Yes, absolutely! This is God's plan. This is what He intended all along. God sent Jesus Christ as not only your substitute, but also your example of how believers around the world can share with others and touch lives.

Space does not allow us to outline all the ways we can touch and influence lives like He did. But know this, as you allow Him to live in you, eventually you will desire more of His life working through you to others. Think about that for a moment. The more you become like Christ, the more you'll live for Christ. You'll begin to see what He sees, feel what He feels, and love as He loves. Jesus touched lives and you will, too.

Jesus Preached and Demonstrated the Kingdom of God

Jesus said, "the Kingdom of God is at hand" (Mark 1:15). This was fantastic news to the Jewish community at that time. They had known about the Kingdom of Israel. They had heard that

God was going to one day restore David's Kingdom. They had eagerly anticipated the day when God would send the Messiah and He would overthrow the Roman government. Was Jesus the Messiah? Was He ushering in the Kingdom they had so long waited for? Could it be true? Yes, and more so.

Jesus' message was the proclamation of God's Kingdom. Jesus told His followers the Kingdom of God was here! He demonstrated that fact by showing the Kingdom's power and presence in many ways: healing the sick, walking on water, casting out demons, and multiplying the bread. We're even told Jesus entered into the region where the "shadow of death" had kept the people in darkness (Matthew 4:16). And upon His entrance the "people saw a great light" (Matthew 4:16) This was the impact of the Kingdom as Jesus entered their presence.

The reason we touch on Jesus' message here is because, as we live like Christ, and for Christ, our message will be His message. You, too, can share, speak, and offer the joy of His Kingdom on this earth. You can carry and demonstrate the presence of His Kingdom by stepping into His anointing and power. You can heal, bless, and see miracles because of the Kingdom's presence on this earth.

Stop and think for a moment about the region and area in which you live. Is there darkness, doubt, fear, or lack? Is there financial hardship, murder, violence, and despair? Are the people hardened to the Kingdom of God and Jesus Christ? If so, it sounds a lot like society in Jesus' day.

And you have the opportunity to make a difference to those around you. But it all starts with your decision.

You have the opportunity to make a difference to those around you. But it all starts with a decision. Yes, a decision to live an inspired life where Jesus' message becomes your message and His mission becomes your assignment.

Jesus Influenced Others to Follow

There was something magnetic about His personality. Jesus Christ's life drew people to Him. He radiated kindness, grace, and inspiration. He attracted people from all walks of life; the rich and the downcast. He never rejected anyone and He actually encouraged everyone to follow Him. And follow they did! Multitudes came to hear Him and to be healed. In fact, in every city and village He visited, the sick and the lame were brought in droves and He healed them.

Jesus drew twelve men to be close to Him and through these men He would build His church. These twelve men, or apostles (minus Judas Iscariot), would go on to rock the world!

They simply took what Jesus taught them and shared His gospel throughout the then known regions of the earth. These men also lived attractive, magnetic lives. Through the power of the Holy Spirit they continued to draw multitudes to Him. And so, down through history the pattern became the same. Believers touched others lives and raised up disciples who, in turn, reached out and continued to touch lives.

What about you? Are you following Christ and are others following because of your influence? You see, the inspired life we're speaking of will inspire others to live for Christ. As Jesus Christ lives in you His presence will be evident in you and others will see it and be drawn to Him, too.

You ask, how can I inspire others to follow Christ? It's simple, just draw close to God and allow Christ to live through you. Yes, ask the Holy Spirit to fill you and live through you as you go about your everyday life. Look for opportunities to share, to bless, and to love others. Look for opportunities to allow God's grace to influence others. And know that Jesus Christ will go before you and open doors to you so that His influence through you will continue to inspire others.

Jesus Knew Where He Was Going

Did you know Jesus was never confused? He never was bewildered or wondering about His future. He didn't worry about where His provision was coming from and He didn't fret about a retirement plan. No, Jesus knew where He was going and He was confident that God the Father had a plan for everything concerning Him. One of the most profound statements Jesus made was:

I know where I came from and where I am going. John 8:14 (NLV)

How is it humanly possible for a man to make such a statement; to know your past and future? Oh, but, this was no ordinary man. This was the God-Man, Jesus Christ. And He could make this statement because of who He was and the relationship He had with His Father.

Jesus had a clear vision of where He came from and where He was going. He knew He could go to the Father, pray, and gain insight as to what the next day held for Him. He knew He could pray and see His Father work on His behalf. Jesus Christ had such a confidence about Him that He could say, "I know where I'm going."

Now here's the profound part. You, too, can make such a

statement. You can say, "I know where I'm going!" As Jesus Christ lives in you there is the working of His Holy Spirit where, as Jesus said:

> When he, the Spirit of truth, comes, he will guide you into all the truth. He will not speak on his own; he will speak only what he hears, and he will tell you what is yet to come. John 16:13 (NIV)

What a promise! Read it again! There before you is the guarantee of the Holy Spirit to live, guide, and direct you just as He led Jesus. Thus, one of the strong characteristics of knowing Jesus Christ is not only to learn how to hear from the Father, overcome challenges, and be an influence to others, but to also have the privilege and promise to be led by Him. Yes, God the Father wants you to be able to say, like His Son, "I know where I'm going." But, this is only possible as you know Him, and as you ask for His Spirit to live in and through you. You, too, can be led by the Lord. You can live an inspired life as you allow God to unfold to you His plan for your future.

In Summary

Living an inspired Christian life begins with knowing Jesus Christ and making a choice to live like Him. And when you choose to live like Him you'll discover that He is your blueprint, He is your template, and He is the example for you. He was led by the Father, obeyed the Father, overcame evil, and was empowered by the Spirit of God. His message was the Kingdom of God and He drew many to follow Him.

Today, you can choose to live like Jesus Christ. Today, His

Spirit is alive and will live in you and give you the ability to influence this earth with His power and Kingdom. This is living the inspired life, friends. To live as Jesus Christ lived has no comparison. It is a life most others would only dream about but it is a life available to all who believe. Pray this prayer today:

> Lord God, thank you for sending Jesus your Son as an example of how I, too, can live. Today I choose to give my life over to you. Speak to me as your son/daughter. Lead me to overcome in every area of life. Fill me with your Spirit in order to share Your Kingdom and draw others to You. Give me the grace to say, like Jesus, "I know where I came from, and where I'm going." AMEN!

Chapter 3

"Follow Me": Answering Your Call to Follow the Master

Follow Me, and I will make you become fishers of men. Mark 1:17

Peter probably remembered very well the day the Rabbi from Nazareth visited the shores of the Sea of Galilee and walked by his boat. "Follow Me" is what he heard from Him. Peter responded, along with his brother, Andrew, and eventually ten other men, and thus the journey of a lifetime began.

Little did Peter know he would go on to live a world changing inspired life. Little did he know his name would be talked about for centuries to come as the man named Simon, who Jesus Christ would refer to as Peter.

What was it that drew Jesus to Simon Peter? What motivated Jesus the Rabbi to extend an invitation to Peter, and the others, to "follow me"? The answer to this question has filled thousands of books over the years. Today, the answer is very simple. God had a plan to call men and women who would turn and follow Him so He could mold, shape, build, and restore His image on the earth. God's plan of salvation centered on His Son Jesus Christ, but it was to be extended throughout the world through men and women like you.

But there was a process of forming His men and women that needed to take place in order for this plan to be successful. Thus we have the call to "follow me."

Today the call is the same. To those who want to learn of Jesus Christ: follow Him. To those who want to live the most amazing, astounding, and exciting life: follow the Rabbi from Nazareth. To the broken-hearted, down-trodden, crushed victims of life, the invitation is: follow Him. To the rich, the poor, the famous, and the powerful: follow Him. The choice, and the only choice that leads to a full life, an empowered life, is the choice to hear His call: "follow Me!"

Follow Me—The Invitation to Unlock Your Purpose

"Follow me," *lech aharai* (literally, "walk after me"), was a technical term in Hebrew for becoming a disciple.[5] So the invitation to "follow me" literally means to "walk after Christ." And thus, we follow, walking in His steps as He leads.

What does it mean to follow Christ? What were Christ's intentions in raising up disciples? What does a disciple or follower of Christ look and act like today? These questions and more will be reviewed as we discover what it means to be a disciple of Christ.

The Discovery of Your Purpose

In Jesus' day, He was recognized as a rabbi with *semikhah*, or with authority.[6] This was the highest level of rabbinical training in Jesus' day and very few men ever received this status. History shows there were no semikhah rabbi in Judea in Christ's day and only a few in Galilee. A semikhah rabbi had the Old Testament

---

[5] Bible Scholars, *"Study Shows Jesus as Rabbi"*, Roy Blizzard and David Bivin, May, 2013 <http://www.biblescholars.org/2013/05/study-shows-jesus-as-rabbi.html>

[6] Berean Bible Church, *"Jesus the Rabbi"*, David Curtis, October, 2006, <http://www.bereanbiblechurch.org/transcripts/mark/9_5.htm>

memorized word for word and was looked to as the authority of Jewish religious activity.

A semikhah rabbi today would be the equivalent of a "Top Gun" pilot, a quarterback of a Super Bowl Team, a winner of an Academy Award or a Grammy, or a President of the United States. In fact, all of these positions and awards would be easier to achieve than becoming a semikhah rabbi. The synagogue was the centerpiece of the Jewish community and the rabbi was honored as a man of God. But a semikhah rabbi was looked upon with the highest level of honor even over the local rabbi. As part of their tradition, when a rabbi received semikhah status he was to go back to the rabbi training schools and pick the brightest, most intelligent, promising students whom he would personally mentor.

Jesus was calling out to the common man.

Now it should be easy for you to understand Peter and Andrew's shock when they heard Jesus say, "follow me." Wow! Jesus didn't pick the top of the class from rabbi school. No, He walked by the sea and picked uneducated fishermen to follow Him and be mentored by Him.

"Are you kidding me? You want me?" perhaps Peter thought. And so was the surprise of the other men and women Jesus selected to follow Him.

Jesus was calling out to the common man. Jesus wasn't looking for the most educated, most eloquent, or most well-off financially, He was looking for common, everyday folk who He could extend an invitation to, to follow Him with the intent of training them to change the world!

Making and Becoming Prepares You for Purpose

Jesus Christ said to Peter and Andrew, "follow Me and I'll make you fishers of men." In saying this, Jesus identified with their occupation and turned what they recognized as their day to day activity and job into their purpose to follow Christ.

Today, if you are a banker Jesus could say, "follow Me and I'll teach you to manage the treasures of men's hearts." If you are a mother with several children, Jesus could say, "follow Me and I'll teach you how to care for the souls of many young ones." Take whatever occupation or status of life you are now in and the invitation is to you, too. Jesus says, "follow Me and I'll take what you do and fill in the blank line with what you were created to be before time began."

Jesus Christ is saying, "follow Me and I'll give you a life of purpose, meaning, and fulfillment. He says He will make you what you were destined for. In Peter's case, he no longer simply caught fish from the sea. No, Peter was taught by the Master how to catch men for God's Kingdom.

What about you? What do you do in life? How can God take what you do and who you are and turn it into an inspired, changed life filled with the purpose you were created for? Listen friends, there is a blank line God will fill in as you walk after Jesus Christ. He says, "follow Me and I will make you become _____!"

What will that blank line be in your life? What will be said about you in the years to come? What is it that Jesus Christ desires to build and mold you into? Whatever it is, based on Jesus' track record, we know it will be life changing, thrilling, exciting, and yes, inspiring. Are you ready for a change? Then read on.

Time Spent With Christ

Let's say the disciples spent twelve hours a day, awake, with the Master. Jesus spent approximately three and half years with these men. Do the math and you find a total of 15,330 hours spent with the Master. If a pastor or leader would spend seven hours a week discipling others it would take them forty-two years to do what Jesus did in three and a half years. Friends, Jesus spent a lot of time training, molding, teaching, shaping, and, we believe, even laughing with His disciples. Listen to Jesus' words again:

Follow Me, and I will make you become… Mark 1:17

Let's take a closer look at the what the Master is saying here because, contained in this phrase "make you become," we will find Jesus' intent to call, not only His original disciples, but also to call you to "walk after Christ."

The phrase, "make you," in the original Greek is *poieo* and speaks of "producing, bringing forth, constructing, to make ready and prepare."[7] It also means to "make something out of nothing." Another meaning is to "declare one anything" or "to be the author of a thing." Thus, Jesus was saying to Peter, "follow Me, and I'll build, construct, and prepare you to be something you previously were not."

The phrase "become," here in this verse, in the Greek is *ginomai* which means "to come into existence, to come to pass, to arise, appear in history, and come upon the stage as men appearing in public." Now, putting these meanings together, we find that Jesus is saying "I will make you rise up at this point in history with the intent of appearing and taking center stage as to

---

[7] Blueletter Bible, quoting Strongs Concordance, number G4160
http://www.blueletterbible.org/lang/lexicon/lexicon.cfm?Strongs=G4160&t=NKJV

your purpose."

So, let's put the invitation of Jesus all together. He said to Peter,

> Walk after Me and I'll mold, shape, build, and make you into something you were not before so that you can rise up and appear at this time in history for God's purpose that He created and is ready to speak over your life. (Chris Cobb's Amplified Version)

Wow! Jesus' intention was much more than Peter just going for a casual walk with Him. Oh no, Jesus called Peter, and He's calling you to rise up and take your place as a follower of Christ. He is calling you to be one who is shaped, conformed, equipped, anointed, and readied to make a lasting, impactful, influence on this earth. Yes, Jesus' calls you to rise up and appear at your appointed time in history so that what you were foreordained to be and do will be seen by Heaven, Hell, and the sphere of life you were called to live in.

Today Jesus is calling for men and women, like you, because He wants to step into their lives. He wants them to spend time with Him so that God's plan can and will be done.

Jesus said, "I will build my Church" (Matthew 16:18) You are a vital part of the building. You are needed to help build. You are invited to join the greatest movement of men and women this world has ever seen.

After the call to "follow Me," the disciples journeys began. One day at a time, Jesus asked the men and women to simply follow Him. Jesus did the leading while His disciples did the following. Jesus Christ knew where He was going and where He was taking His disciples.

The essence of following Christ is simply spending time with Him.

Day by day, Jesus was the classroom. He was the textbook. One lesson at a time. One miracle watched. One parable at a time. The gospels show that for approximately the first year, Jesus did most everything. The disciples watched, learned, asked questions, and were basically blown away by what they saw.

Jesus demonstrated the Father's heart and the power of the Kingdom in their presence. These men and women saw Jesus stare down demons, confront the religious system, and change the molecular structure of water into wine. They witnessed first hand fish multiplied, blind eyes opened, the crippled healed, and even Jesus defying the laws of nature as He used the sea as a sidewalk.

The essence of following Christ at the beginning was simply spending time with Him. So, the first action on our part, after we answer the call to follow, is to simply spend time with Christ. This involves asking many questions, hearing from Him, allowing Him to teach us and correct us, and so forth. This is why Bible study small groups, and being a part of a local church are essential to the modern day growth of a disciple.

Three Stages of Spiritual Maturity

Just like a little child is born and begins to grow and develop, a new follower of Christ is "birthed" into a new life and begins growing. A person who makes the decision to follow Christ is not born a mature, fully grown believer over night. No, just like a little child, there will be times when you learn to crawl, then walk, and then you finally run.

You are first given the nourishment and food that a spiritual child would eat. This includes learning to pray and read your Bible everyday as well as the lessons and teachings from adult believers. Then, as you mature, you can handle the food that a spiritual adult eats like some of the deeper doctrines and ministry to others. And so, this analogy can be developed and applied to every new follower of Christ.

John the Apostle gives us insight to this truth when he lays before us, by the Holy Spirit, certain characteristics of our maturing process. John tells us:

> I write to you, fathers, because you have known Him who is from the beginning. I write to you, young men, because you have overcome the wicked one. I write to you, little children, because you have known the Father…
> 1 John 2:13

Spiritual Infancy

John talks about little children, meaning spiritual infants. Babies are cute and cuddly! There is no shame at all in being a little baby. The difficulty is when we stay there. Just as we grow into adults physically and mentally, we need to move past spiritual infancy in our walk with Christ. Paul encourages believers to not stay as a child, but to continue to grow into maturity in Christ:

> It's like this: when I was a child I spoke and thought and reasoned as a child does. But when I became a man my thoughts grew far beyond those of my childhood, and now I have put away the childish things. 1 Corinthians

13:11 (TLB).

Babies are totally dependent on others and vulnerable to life's dangers. A baby believer depends on others for prayer, guidance, and is vulnerable to spiritual dangers. Paul admonishes:

> [When we are fully grown in the Lord] we will no longer be immature like children. We won't be tossed and blown about by every wind of new teaching. We will not be influenced when people try to trick us… Ephesians 4:14 (NLT).

Babies are also selfish and messy. A baby cries to get what it wants. A baby believer is also selfish and messy. They pray for themselves, and think and live for themselves. The spiritually immature are vulnerable and self-focused.

Even though babies are cute, they are not ready for the more mature lifestyle and responsibilities of an adult, such as driving a car, going to college, or getting married. In the same way, baby believers are not ready for the responsibilities of a spiritual adult, such full-time ministry, or pastoring a church.

Spiritual Adolescence

The term "young men" is generic, meaning believers who are at the spiritual adolescent stage. They are getting stronger and making progress in their Christian lives, but they are also not yet ready for the greater tasks and responsibilities of a mature Christian.

What is a spiritual adolescent? Adolescence is the transition time between infancy and full maturity. It's the stage where we learn to control ourselves, handle responsibility, and learn to say "no."

Adolescents are flushed with overconfidence and under-experience. They goof up, make mistakes, and, hopefully they learn from them. As adolescents, we come into strength and learn our limits instead of always pushing past them.

Spiritual adolescents pray for strength, run after strength, and show off their strength. They are strong and inspired. They're at a great stage of spiritual growth, but they are not yet fully mature.

> The glory of young men is their strength: and the beauty of old men is the grey head. Proverbs 20:29 (KJV).

Spiritual Maturity

Under Roman law, there was a time for the coming of age of a son. A Roman child became an adult at a festival known as the *Liberalia* held every year on March 17th. On that day, a father recognized his son as his heir, and the son received the garment of an adult. Each of us is called to grow to the place where we can wear a garment of spiritual maturity.

> Therefore let us leave the elementary teachings about Christ and go on to maturity… Hebrews 6:1 (NIV).

How can you tell if you're at this level? You're there when you have fully embraced the rights and responsibilities of the Kingdom of God. The mature Christians have moved past being messy, selfish, and unproven. They are using their lives for the glory of God. They pray for others, live for others, and duplicate Christ in others. What stage of growth are you in?

What is a Disciple of Christ Called to Do?

A disciple of Christ? What do they do? How do they live out their Christian life? What activities are they involved in? Is being a disciple more than joining a church and getting baptized? Is living as a disciple of Christ more than going to a Bible study, saying daily prayers, or helping to feed the homeless? While there are many church activities a person may be involved in, do they qualify a person to be a true follower of the Master?

Let's begin our discussion on this subject by evaluating three basic fundamentals we find in scripture which very simply outline for us what it means to be a disciple of Christ.

1. You're Called to Follow Him

One of first things Jesus Christ did when His ministry began was to call men and women to follow Him. There are about fifty-nine references in the gospels to people following Christ. Jesus issued forth the call and people responded. So, the first priority of Christ was to call others around Him. He said,

Follow Me... Mark 1:17

Now, many "followed" Christ for a variety of reasons and motives. Some followed Him for the miracles, many followed Him because of the meals He fed them, But there were some who followed and continued to learn from Him. They grew as true followers, or disciples of Christ. What follows are a number of expectations, and overall characteristics of a person who is wholly devoted to following Christ.

- **The Invitation to Follow.** Jesus Christ's call went out to all people and is still going forth today. Jesus said, "whoever comes to me I will in no way reject" (John 6:37).

- **The Fellowship of Following.** Jesus said, "come to me all you who are weary and burdened and I will give you rest" (Matthew 11:30). As we follow Christ, He truly does give the weary soul rest and peace. This is a wonderful promise to those who follow and come into fellowship with Him. Jesus said, "I stand at the door... and if anyone opens I will come in and fellowship with him (or her)" (Revelation 3:20).

- **The Training, Teaching, and Mentoring.** Jesus was, and still is, the consummate teacher. He spent much time teaching, imparting, mentoring, correcting, and inspiring His disciples. He wasted no life situation from which to share and teach. His pattern was to find a life situation, explain it in the context of the Kingdom, and then add a couple of parables for reinforcement. After teaching, the Master would then ask, "have you understood all things?" (Matthew 13:51)

- **The Total Commitment.** Jesus expects a total surrender to Him in every area of our lives. He said we are to love the Lord God with all our heart, mind, soul, and spirit (Matthew 22:37). And if we love Him, then He expects us to keep His commandments (John 14:15). The Apostle Peter's commitment was strong and final as seen in his statement, "We must obey God rather than men" (Acts 5:29).

- **The Cost of Following.** A fully devoted follower of Christ needs to know and understand the cost of being a disciple. Yes, it will cost you to follow Christ. Some tough choices need to be made in order to fully and completely follow Him.

Even as Jesus carried a cross, He said we, too, will have a cross to carry. Jesus said we must take up our cross daily and follow Him (Luke 9:23). The cross for a believer is sometimes a choice concerning a family, a job, past habits, and hang ups. The Apostle Paul put it this way when he said, "I have been crucified with Christ and I no longer live, but Christ lives in me. The life I now live in the body, I live by faith in the Son of God, who loved me and gave himself for me" (Galatians 2:20).

- **The Equipping of the Disciple.** Jesus did not leave His disciples powerless. Jesus anointed and equipped them to live in a realm of victory never before seen on this earth. Jesus gave His disciples the power to heal the sick, cast out demons, the authority to pray, and even raise the dead (Matthew 10:1). Jesus later baptized His disciples with His Holy Spirit and thus, they had the necessary empowerment to fulfill what He had called them to be and do (Acts 1:8).

- **The Sending of the Disciple.** Jesus never intended for His disciples to keep His gospel to themselves. There came a day in their training when He sent them out to do the very same things He had done. Jesus said, "as the Father has sent me, I am sending you" (John 20:21). The follower is now being sent to represent the Master. We now have, as followers of Christ, the responsibility to continue on with His message, His agenda, and His mission. The Bible says we are ambassadors of His Kingdom (2 Corinthians 5:20). Know this, that as you follow Christ, there will come a time when you will be sent out for Christ. To continue to share His gospel is a natural byproduct of our commitment to Him.

Jesus was very intentional about calling people to Himself with the plan of making, molding, and shaping them for His Kingdom. But as a starting point, you are invited to follow and commit all of your life to Him. Yes, Jesus expects total obedience and commitment from you. There is a saying that goes, "If Jesus is not Lord of all, He's not Lord at all."

2. You are Commanded to Love

Jesus Christ was sitting with His men at the table of the last supper. In this setting, a final command was issued which was,

> A new command I give you: Love one another. John 13:34

Jesus goes on to say that the world would know they are His disciples by walking in love (John 13:35). So, in one sentence, Jesus summed up the one thing that would differentiate them from everyone else, and that was love for each other.

Jesus commanded us to love one another. Jesus Christ desires, and even demands, that we learn how to get along, and truly love each other in order to be one of His. Jesus then went on to show the extent of what this love is when He said,

> There is no greater love than to lay down one's life for one's friends. John 15:13

There are many "believers" in the church world who say they are a disciple of Christ, yet they harbor bitterness, animosity, and resentment towards one another. It is amazing to me how many "Christians" will say they worship God, yet in their heart they don't have the kind of love that Jesus is expecting from them.

> *It's time for a heart check. We need to ask the Lord to reveal areas in our lives where we are not walking in love.*

So for many of us, it's time for a heart check. We need to check our hearts and ask the Lord to reveal areas in our lives where we are not walking in love. To say we love the Lord and yet we don't love others is hypocritical and deceptive. Now consider the following additional areas where we are to show love to others as well.

- **Love Your Enemies.** Jesus said we're to love even our enemies (Matthew 5:44). How can we fulfill this command? We can't unless we obey the Master and allow Him to love through us. "Our enemies" include our family and loved ones who have hurt us. They include those around us who have betrayed and abandoned us. They even include those closest to you who you trusted yet they let you down.

- **Love Your Neighbor as Yourself.** Jesus makes clear His expectations of the quality of love we are to show others. That love is compared to how you would like to be treated. Jesus said, "do to others what you would have them do to you" (Luke 6:31). You desire to be respected, honored, not lied about, and trusted. Even so, you then love, honor, and respect "your neighbor," co-worker, or anyone else close to you.

- **Love Your Brother and Sister.** The Bible is clear: we are to be kindly affectionate to one another with brotherly love (Romans 12:10). This love will be seen in how we encourage one another, wait on one another, prefer one another, and honor one another.

- **Love for the Lost.** When you come to Christ, it won't be long before the same love that was extended to you begins to fill your heart for those around you who don't know Christ. Love for the lost in this world is a natural outflow of the love of Christ in your life. The Apostle Paul went so far as to say it was the love of Christ that motivated him to fulfill his ministry (2 Corinthians 5:14). Yes, and you, too, can experience God's love for this world and for those living without Him. This can be difficult at times when we think of all the unloving people in this world. Listen to some Christians and you can quickly tell if there is a critical, cynical spirit within them towards certain types of people. Or, it will be clear that they have the compassion of Christ for those destined to eternal suffering and anguish if they don't repent and turn their life over to Him.

3. You have a Responsibility to Reach

All authority has been given to Me in heaven and on earth. Go therefore and make disciples of all the nations…
(The Great Commission) Matthew 28:18-19

One of the strong characteristics of a follower of Christ is the desire to reach out with His love to those around and offer them a new life in Him. As mentioned in the previous section, a truly devoted follower of Christ cannot help but have the love of Christ in them that wants to reach out to this world. In fact, there is a non-negotiable command from our Lord to "go therefore." So a disciple, a follower of Christ, recognizes the Master's directive and looks for ways and means to engage in this world with His salvation.

Compare this to many who are in the church who say they

love the Lord, and even love their brother or sister in Christ. But take a closer look at their life and you may see very little fruit of what Jesus said in the Great Commission. Friends, we are to take this very seriously and it is deceptive to say we love God when we don't reach out to the lost.

Then there are many in the church who truly desire to love the Lord and love others, but they have never been shown how to reach out to the lost. There are many who have never been mentored, taught, or shown how easy it is to live an inspired life and give away their faith to the world.

In fact, most Christians are in this category. For when we speak of outreach, witnessing, or sharing, the American church has certain predisposed, historical characteristics that may limit a believer's opportunities to share with the lost. We firmly believe, however, that to share Christ with hungry, hurting people is one of the easiest and blessed ministries we can enter into. You see friends, we have at our disposal the greatest story ever told. We have the power to change the lives, and histories, of those God puts in front of us. Many times it is God Himself who goes before us to set up divine appointments so that we can bring light into the dark places in other people's lives.

I'm convinced that most of the church in America, if mentored on how to simply pray and reach out, would step up and step into others people's lives with Christ's love.

Is there going to be rejection? Yes. Will there be those who resist, want to argue, and shut you down? Yes. But there are those who truly do want to know about Christ's love and the inspired life and perhaps no one has ever taken the time to love them, not judge them, and simply share the gospel of Christ with them.

> *82% of people in America would visit a local church when asked. But then again only about 2% of church members ever ask!*

Consider the statistic that 82% of people in America would visit a local church when asked.[8] But then again only 2% of church members ever ask! That is staggering because it shows that we assume people would come to church, know Christ and get "saved" if they wanted to, but they don't. The reality is that there are many out there in the world searching, hurting, and desiring to know truth.

Tim Keller

Tim Keller, the pastor of Redeemer Church in downtown Manhattan, in the heart of New York City, has openly stated that many believe America, and New York, is turned off to the gospel of Christ. But this is not his experience at all. He's found there are thousands in the heart of New York who are truly desiring to know God. But who are the ones who will risk their time and reputation to reach out to them?

In Summary

Let's review what we've covered thus far. We said that a disciple is a follower of Christ. We went on to explain that a disciple loves God and loves others. And lastly, we've stated that a disciple reaches out to others following Jesus' command.

---

[8] National Back to Church Sunday, Participant resources, 2015 http://backtochurch.com/participate/resources/statistics/

Therefore, let us summarize in one sentence what a disciple is:

A disciple is a follower of Christ who loves God, loves others, and reaches out to the lost.

Can you pass the test of true discipleship?

This is a very easy test, but it will challenge you to the very core of your life and being. The test asks three questions:

1. Do you follow Christ?
2. Do you love God and others?
3. Do you reach out to the lost with God's love and salvation?

If you said yes to all of the above questions then you qualify as a true disciple of Christ.

You'd be surprised to find there are scores of professing Christians who say they love and follow Christ, yet they have little patience and lack of love toward others. Then there are cultural Christians who go to church for friends, fellowship, and, perhaps, food but following, obeying, and trusting God with all their hearts is not a top priority. Lastly, there many who say they follow Christ and love others, but when asked about their efforts to share and reach out to the lost, you'll find some blank stares looking back at you.

Friends, God is looking for true disciples. He is looking for more than church membership and social, cultural "believers." God is yearning to draw men and women into a relationship with Him called "disciple" whereby He can fill, anoint, and live an inspired life through them. The most powerful, inspirational, and impactful people walking the earth today are true "followers" of Christ. These are His disciples. And these disciples are continuing to fulfill His plan and Kingdom rule on this earth.

Remember, Jesus Christ's agenda hasn't changed for over 2,000 years. He's saying today, as He did long ago, "follow Me." And if you say "yes," and respond to His call, you, too, can join the ranks of millions before us who "follow Him, "love others," and "reach out" to this world. This is what a disciple does. You can be one, too! Have you said "yes" to His call? If so, then go and live it out. Inspire someone today!

Chapter 4

Relationships: The Power and Purpose of Living Connected

God said, "It's not good for the Man to be alone." Genesis 2:18

In our discussions of living the inspired life, we also want to speak of inspired lives, plural. Plural, in that God never intended for men and women to live, work, and carry out their lives alone. Why was this? Because God created mankind to live connected to others; in their relationships, their family, and in their generations to come.

Yes, God intended for His people to live in a relationship with others for specific purposes. These purposes being to receive and reflect the potential of His inspired life in and through His family and their relationships.

From the very beginning Adam and Eve were to be connected, fruitful, and multiply. They were to birth a family and a generation which was in covenant relationship with the Lord. Of course, we know the result of Adam's sin and how it affected families down through time. But God had a plan to restore and reconnect His people to Himself. He had a plan to display before all creation the power of an inspired family.

God's call to Abraham reflects His desire to draw and connect families back to Himself. God said to Abraham, "in you all the families of the earth shall be blessed" (Genesis 12:3). And down through time we read in the Bible that God continued to work through relationships and families for the purpose of establishing His covenant on this earth.

Online Dating

Have you noticed the boom in online dating recently? Online dating has surpassed all forms of matchmaking in the United States, other than friends and family, according to the latest research. Sites like Match.com, eHarmony, and Christian Mingle are a boon to nearly thirty million lonely-hearted people every month, largely because their software automates the task of finding a perfect match. There used to be a stigma against all this (I'd ask couples how they met, and they'd look sheepish and whisper, "We met online.") but it's fading. Whatever your view, there's no denying that people are created with a need for a perfect connection.

Why is this topic added as a whole chapter in a book on living an inspired life? Because we have before us, in this day and age, a culture driving a wedge through our marriages, families, and churches that will affect the generations to come.

Robert Puttman, a Harvard scholar, wrote in his book *Bowling Alone*, that in America we are seeing a decline of people connecting with each other. Puttman points out that in almost every segment of society, over the past seventy-five years now, people are becoming more and more isolated from one another. Thus creating a vacuum in our society of empty, lonely, and depressed people. In fact, he said, "if you want to see a quintessential example of individualism today look no further than Silicon Valley of the Bay Area."

Today we are seeing the effects of individualism in our

families, marriages, relationships, and even in the church. Yes, the relationships and families in the church are, many times, no different than in the secular world. The aftermath of individualism is seen in the breakdown of marriages and family relationships. Never before in our land and church have we witnessed such loneliness, despair, anxiety, isolation, and depression. Never before have we seen such fractured relationships, rejection, betrayal, and loss of hope between family members. But God's grace is available to restore the family.

As you read through this chapter, our goal is for you to discover the wonderful potential of God stepping into your relationships. He will begin to restore His original plan of connecting people with people. His plan includes fathers and mothers, friends, relatives, co-workers, neighbors, grandparents, cousins, etc. You see, God works through people, for people.

His plan is to bless the generations to come. We're told in the Bible that God desires to "show love to a thousand generations of those who love me and keep my commandments" (Exodus 20:4). It is through the family and covenant relationships that God looks to build up a people who will join together for His common purpose, and inspire His grace on this earth. As we walk together in His love and purpose, we will be the blueprints of His family living on this earth. We can inspire others as to what is available for them on this earth today and what Heaven will be like tomorrow!

The Inspired Life is Lived Out in Relationships

> Behold, how good and how pleasant it is for brethren to dwell together in unity! ...for there the LORD commanded the blessing, even life forevermore. Psalms 133:1,3 (KJV)

This psalm is abundantly clear: when we come together in unity, it's good and pleasant. God releases an anointing. He looses and commands a blessing. This is why we are encouraged repeatedly throughout the New Testament to keep the unity of our faith and not allow disunity to dwell within a local church. God desires you to have a relationship with Him and with those around you. And in so doing, you can expect His promise of the commanded blessing to be present.

9/11 Phone Calls

When passengers aboard the hijacked 9/11 planes saw they wouldn't make it, several reached for their cell phones and dialed their loved ones. Their final words were things like: *"I love you...I'm glad I married you...Tell the kids Daddy loves them."* They could have said, *"Don't forget to water the lawn"* or *"Take care of my car."* But they focused on relationships. Why do you suppose that is?

Relationships are Key to Everything We Do In Life

Relationships are key to everything we do in life: our accomplishments, victories, recovering from failure, warmth, protection, and security. These are awesome powers working in relationships. Relationships are powerful because they are spiritual. Relationships always involve the exchange of spirit which affects our attitudes, beliefs, morality, and ethics. When you have strong, blessed relationships there will be the exchange of God's grace for everyone to share in.

Relationships are key to everything we do in life . . . relationships are powerful

When God's commanded blessing is present and shared, everyone is blessed. We are blessed with God's presence, His love, forgiveness, strength, hope, and faith. Miracles can be expected in every area of life when His commanded blessing is present. This is why it is vital that you understand and receive the benefit of the power of relationships. It is in the power of these relationships that the inspired life is shared among the many in the church and in the family.

A powerful example of the strength of God's commanded blessing is seen when the people of Israel were about to enter the promised land. During their journey Balaam was hired by Balak, King of Moab, to curse Israel (Numbers 22). Balaam returned from his assignment having failed because he said,

> The LORD his God *is* with him, and the shout of a King *is* among them. Numbers 23:21

Balaam couldn't curse Israel because God was with them and in their midst. This is an example of the power of the commanded blessing. This is what we want and need today: God's presence in our midst. And God is looking for a home, a family, and a church where His people live together in unity. When He finds this, He commands His blessing. This is the power of relationships living the inspired life—together.

Six Healthy Relationships of an Inspired Life

1. Relationship with Jesus Christ

The first and most important relationship you need is between you and Jesus Christ. Even though we've mentioned this before, let's go a little deeper in explaining the depth of this relationship.

When you are born again the Spirit of God is poured into your life and a wonderful transformation takes place. You have a new identity and are now positioned to find God's overall purpose in your life. The Spirit of God enters your life and you become "one" with Christ. The Bible says you are now "bone of His bone and flesh of His flesh" (Ephesians 5:30). This means you are vitally connected to Christ as He fills your life. You may not have felt any different at first, but nevertheless, Heaven listened and drew you into a very real relationship with Jesus Christ.

The Bible speaks of this relationship with Jesus as "Christ in you" (Colossians 1:27). This is Christ in you; filling, molding, motivating, leading, and guiding you. His Spirit is living you. It is now a reality where you hear His thoughts, know what's on His mind, and you are "one with Him."

The phrase "temple of the Holy Spirit" takes on a new meaning in that your body and soul, wall to wall, become filled with His presence, anointing, and power. The Bible says you are the dwelling place of God by His Spirit (1 Corinthians 3:16, 6:19 and 2 Corinthians 6:16). Yes, God lives in you and you become the carrier of God's presence on this earth. Just think, wherever you go, God goes. He lives in you and walks with you, saturating every cell and fiber of your being.

Now you are never alone. This is why Jesus can say, "I will never leave you or forsake you" (Hebrews 13:5). Because He lives in you. Now, it's up to you to allow God to fill your life.

The Bible speaks of a desire to be continually filled with His Spirit (Ephesians 5:18). The original language here speaks of a "continual" filling.⁹ So, today you can be filled with His Spirit, and then tomorrow you can ask the Father for more of His Spirit. You can receive a fresh anointing and outpouring on a daily basis.

God is looking for people He can fill with His Spirit. He is looking for people who will demonstrate to this earth who He is. Yes, you can walk and live on this earth as He walked and lived because of the presence of Jesus living in you by His Holy Spirit. Jesus said, "at that day you will know that I am in My Father and you in me, and I in you" (John 14:20). Truly friends, we can become one with Him, connected to Him, and live out an inspired life because He lives in us.

2. Relationship with His Family—The Church

God sets the solitary in families... Psalms 68:6

For many people the mention of church immediately creates a picture of a building with a steeple, a pipe organ, and men and women dressed in their Sunday best listening to a sermon. For many, church is something you do on Sundays where you enter a building, sing a few songs or hymns, listen to a preacher, and then leave one to two hours later to go back home for a Sunday meal and watch the football game.

When Jesus said, "I will build my church" (Matthew 16:18) was He speaking of a building with a steeple or pews? Or did He have something else in mind? The word "church" here is *ekklesia* which literally means "a gathering of people to form an assembly."[10] So, we can rephrase Jesus' statement to mean, "I will

---

[9] The parsing of the verb *pleroo* is in the present, passive, imperative form which speaks of the subject commanded to do now . . . be filled continually (Chris Cobb)

[10] Blueletter Bible, quoting Strongs, number G1392

build and assemble my called out ones." What did Christ have in mind in building His church—His people?

The Bible refers to believers in Christ as His body on this earth. Yes, we, as believers in Christ, form His body and represent Him on this earth. He is the head of His body. We are told that:

> The church is Christ's body, in which he speaks and acts, by which he fills everything with his presence. Ephesians 1:23 (MSG)

Further, the church is:
...a holy temple built by God, all of us built into it, a temple in which God is quite at home. Ephesians 2:22 (MSG).

God's purpose in creating the church is to have a place to live on this earth. Yes, He lives in, and through, us as we gather as His church. You see friends, it is His church, as His representative, which is to be the source of light, grace, and love for their community, city, and the world.

It is His connected members who gather to worship and celebrate Him. It is the gathering of His people together that makes up His body. It is His church that is to show a lost and dying world the power of forgiveness, healing, and salvation. This is why it is vital that we, as members of His church, learn what it means to be connected to each other. It is vital that we live out His presence on this earth. The Bible says:

> The whole body depends on Christ, and all the parts of

<http://www.blueletterbible.org/lang/lexicon/lexicon.cfm?Strongs=G1392&t=KJV>

the body are joined and held together. Each part does its own work to make the whole body grow and be strong with love. Ephesians 4:16

"One Another" Commands

Throughout the New Testament we find fifty-nine "one another" verses. These are statements, directives, and guidelines whereby members of the body of Christ are taught and encouraged to connect with each other. For example, we are told to love, honor, serve, greet, forgive, submit, encourage, pray, and build up "one-another." All these directives are needed so we can learn how to get along and allow God's Spirit to join us together in unity.

> *As we come together in unity, we become His representatives on this earth.*

As a local church fellowship knows and grows in the above truth, a transformation takes place and God's presence will fill His people—the church. The Bible says, "now you are the body of Christ" (1 Corinthians 1:27). As we come together in unity, and of one mind, we become His representatives on this earth. Thus we are able to be the light shining on a hill to a local community and neighborhood. Suffice it to say, God is looking to restore a vital connection with His people so His presence can fill this earth. The Bible says, "as truly as I live all the earth shall be filled with my glory" (Numbers 14:21). God desires to use His body as the agent through which He fills every city, village, country, and nation as His people come, connect, and become a reflection of Him.

The Power of a Small Group of Believers

The early church grew rapidly within the Roman Empire. Within the first three hundred years after Jesus' resurrection, we're told that the total number of Christians in the Roman Empire exceeded 15 million.[11] Yet, this was accomplished with very few "church buildings" at that time. Where did the early church meet? They met in homes! There were thousands of small home groups meeting within cities and the outlying countryside.

Even today, the incredible power of believers meeting in small groups is seen around the world. The fastest growing and strongest body of believers are still meeting in homes. And in most of the world there are very large church buildings where believers meet to celebrate and worship on Sunday. So today, both go hand in hand; the local church building for Sunday gathering, and the small group Bible study during the week, where disciples meet, love, pray, and grow together.

God is using small groups of believers today to make significant impacts and inspire whole communities. One of the signs of a healthy, small, discipleship group is the ongoing outreach to those who don't know Christ. Every time these groups get together there is prayer for their lost friends and relatives, along with plans to connect with them and introduce them to Christ.

Many discipleship groups become very creative in how they connect with the unsaved ones. One group hosts summer beach parties, another group simply invites unsaved friends over for a potluck. Some groups travel, watch a movie, or attend an event. The bottom line is that the intent of small groups is to connect, reach out, and introduce Jesus Christ.

---

[11] Scaruffi.com, *"A Time-Line of the Roman Empire"* Peio Scaruffi, 1999 http://www.scaruffi.com/politics/romans.html

3. Relationship - in Marriage

"Therefore what God has joined together, let not man separate." Matthew 19:6

God created the opportunity for a man and a woman to be joined in a marriage relationship. This relationship, other than our personal relationship with the Lord Jesus Christ, is the highest expression of love and commitment between two individuals on this earth. This love relationship between a husband and wife is a wonderful picture of God's love for us (Ephesians 5:22-33).

Paul's letter to the church at Ephesus portrays a love relationship between Christ and His church—the body of Christ. As Christ connected to His church, "He loved the church and gave Himself for it" (Ephesians 5:25). Even so marriage is the highest form of a male and female connection—loving, giving, and sharing of life together. The Bible says a husband and wife are to be heirs together of the grace of life (1 Peter 3:7).

Incredible power and blessing awaits a couple who learn how to agree in prayer.

In addition to marriage being the highest expression of Christ's love for us, there are number of additional blessings and promises within the marriage covenant.

- **Friendship of Two Individuals Sharing Life Together.** When "two become one" in a marriage relationship, there is the potential for two individuals to completely and totally enjoy one another, have fellowship one with another, and share life together.

- **Physical Enjoyment.** God created a husband and wife to enjoy sexual, physical intimacy. Love is shared emotionally, physically, and spiritually. The two become one as a blessed union and gift from the Lord.

- **Reproductive Fruitfulness.** One of the reasons God created the marriage relationship is to provide a means for children to be born, and thus God allows His blessings to come upon many generations. The Bible says God is seeking Godly offspring through marriage relationships (Malachi 2:15).

- **Responsible Protection.** A husband fulfills his role by laying down his life for his wife and family just as Christ did for the church (Ephesians 5:25).

- **Grow Old Together With God's Blessing.** The Bible has much to say about family blessing handed down through the generations. We're told that the generations of the upright will be blessed (Psalms 112:2). It is God's blessing on a marriage that will inspire the generations to come.

- **The Power of Prayer.** The Bible teaches us that if two people agree on anything when they ask for it in prayer it will be done (Matthew 18:19). Incredible power and blessing awaits a couple who learn how to agree in prayer. The impossible family situations now become possible. In fact, studies show that when a husband and wife pray together, the divorce rate drops, there is harmony in the family, and a long, happy life is available because they agree.

In a marriage, two people become one (Mark 10:8). This is a mystery just as Christ and His body are a mystery. Yet, for those who have experienced and enjoy a blessed marriage relationship, there is the witness within of the blessing of God. Two unique individuals can truly give of themselves to support, bless, help, provide, care, and walk through everyday life experiences together.

All too often, however, many people in a marriage relationship have never realized the depth of blessing available to them. The divorce rate, domestic violence statistics, and studies on the fatherless all point to a society where there are more people who want to get out of a marriage then those who want to stay in.

Today there is a huge void between God's original plan and that which we see across our country's landscape. Space does not allow for a discussion on these points. But suffice it say, a married couple, when joined together before God, can make the choice to live in a blessed, inspired connection.

There are many excellent books, study guides, and pastoral counselors who can give couples the necessary tools to be healed, whole, and grow in a blessed marriage. It is possible to live on this earth, and in this country, and still be an example of an inspired married couple. It is possible for a husband and wife to come together, become one, and set an example others can follow in order to be a reflection of God's plan. Yes, God does have a plan for a man and a woman in marriage. God set the plan in motion when He told Adam and Eve to:

Be fruitful and increase in number; fill the earth and subdue it. Genesis 1:28 (NIV)

This directive was to Adam and Eve. They were to partner

together, as one before God, and be blessed together in the Garden of Eden. Is this blessing still available today? Yes, it is. If a couple is willing to place Jesus Christ as their Lord, first and foremost, and obey His commands, then they can receive His promises.

If you are married, then choose today to live in harmony with your spouse and be blessed before God. If necessary, get some help in order to learn the skills and habits you can use to meet the needs of your mate. But know this, God wants husbands and wives connected. God desires for men and women to come together and enjoy life together—connected.

4. Relationships – in Our Families

There is currently a war raging across our land within the family unit. There are many casualties and losses as the battle continues against parents, teens, kids, and even the little babies. Is all lost? No! There is hope for families. There is help, support, training, and opportunities for families to rebuild. There is hope to restore God's plan to bless and grow His family.

There are reams of data showing the results of broken, damaged, and abandoned families. The destructive patterns usually start when a family is formed without a proper foundation. We're speaking of a marriage that perhaps began with a dream but, for a variety of reasons, never matured into a healthy relationship. We're speaking of kids with a lack of parenting because they were born out of wedlock. Or because a parent abandoned them for any number of other reasons. We're also speaking of many homes where domestic violence, abuse, drugs, and alcohol take its devastating toll over the years.

What do parents, a husband, or a wife do in today's society in order to see God's plan of a blessed family? Where do you begin if you are a parent or a spouse and there are battle scars from the past that interfere and challenge you to raise a Godly family? We suggest you start by making a decision. Yes, the same decision Joshua made a long time ago when he was faced with the same challenges. It was a decision he needed to make for his own family. Joshua, the leader of Israel, as they entered the promised land, boldly stood and declared:

> As for me and my family, we will serve the LORD. Joshua 24:15

You can make this same declaration over your family. This is where family connection, restoration, and rebuilding begins: with a decision to serve the Lord. When you make Jesus Christ the centerpiece and the rock of your family, then the potential of His "family" promises become available to you. Yes, there are many promises God will keep for the family who chooses to put Him first.

God said to Abraham, "in you all the families of the earth shall be blessed" (Genesis 12:3). God's plan was to start with Abraham and begin a family restoration process culminating in Jesus Christ who breaks the power of division and destruction over the family. God further told Israel that His plan was to bless families down to thousands of generations (Exodus 20:4). Just by looking at these two promises we can easily understand that God is not only interested in your family life, but He desires to empower, build, and display His grace and glory over your family unit for years to come.

But once you make the decision to serve the Lord, how do you begin to appropriate God's promise of blessing in the family? Let us suggest a few principles which will help lay a foundation upon which you can establish a connected and blessed family.

Help for the Marriage

As the marriage goes, so goes the family. If a husband and wife will invest in their marriage, then the fruit of a blessed family will be the natural return. It takes time, effort, and commitment for a husband and wife to work on their marriage and build it upon God's word and principles. A blessed family begins with a blessed marriage.

A husband knows and takes responsibility for his role and the wife does likewise. In so doing, they both become one in marriage and lay the ground work for a family to grow strong. Studies show a healthy marriage is the result of a husband and wife spending anywhere between ten to fifteen hours a week together, caring for one another, meeting each others emotional needs, and sharing life together.

The number one reason for marriage failure today is the husband and wife not taking the time together within their marriage. It's that simple. Of course, the work schedule, child demands, and house chores all need to be done, but if a family and marriage is to grow strong and healthy, then a decision needs to be made by the husband and wife to commit the time to make it work.

Help for the Parents

Most parents raise up their kids using the same methods, habits, and skills imparted to them when they were raised by their parents. They do what comes naturally. And, if there were harmful, abusive, and destructive parenting patterns in the previous generation, more than likely those same harmful and abusive patterns will continue down through the generations. These patterns can be broken by a decision to build a foundation of parenting founded on God's word. The Bible says to "train up a child in the way he (or she) should go" (Proverbs 22:6). It is the training, guiding, and teaching from parents, based on scriptural principles, that will correct abusive outbursts, harsh and harmful words, and neglectful habits found in many homes.

If you, the reader, are a parent of a child or children, how are you doing with your parenting skills? Did you come from a generation of harmful and hurtful parenting practices? Have you read or attended any parenting classes based on God's word?

Parents, now is the time to get help and invest in your ability to raise a Godly family. Even if your kids are teens, or in college, there is still time to learn the Biblical patterns of blessing within the family. The Bible says; "all your children shall be taught of the Lord and great shall be their peace" (Isaiah 54:13). The key thought in this promise is the teaching of your children. So take the time to learn how to do it right.

Creating Family Legacies

Friends and family members, it is possible in this day and age to have a blessed, connected, and thriving family. The Bible even promises:

> Happy are those who respect the LORD, who want what he commands. Their descendants will be powerful in the land; the children of honest people will be blessed. Psalms 112:1-2 (NCV)

What a powerful promise. God is ready to stand behind this promise and make it a reality in your family's life when you are devoted to His purpose and plan. It is possible to have a blessed marriage and a family where there is His peace, joy, purpose, and presence. It is possible for parents to know how to raise kids that aren't crazy, strung out on drugs, or rebelling before their teen years. It is possible to raise a family that reflects the glory of God, honors parents, and honors siblings. A family today can commit to prayer and devotional times and overcome the temptations and allurements of this age. It is possible for a family to impact and inspire a neighborhood, a community, and even a generation.

Take the necessary steps needed so Jesus Christ can use your family to inspire the generations to come.

If you are a parent, a member of a family, or someday desire to start a family, then make the decision to build your family on God's word. Take the necessary steps needed so Jesus Christ can, not only bless your family, but cause your family to inspire the generations to come.

5. Relationships – With Our Friends

"There is a friend who sticks closer than a brother." Pro. 18:24

We need friends. We need others in our life whom we can trust, share, and encourage when needed. As the Bible says,

"Two are better than one, . . . for if they fall, one will lift up his companion. But woe to him who is alone when he falls, for he has no one to help him up." Ecc. 4:9-10

There is strength in godly friendships. But the Bible warns there is danger if a person stands alone. Endeavor to find a friend you can bless and who blesses you. Make it your aim in life to have a few close friends with whom you can share life, encouragement and inspiration. Take a close look at the life of Jesus and you will find that He shared His inspiring life with a few close friends. He was a friend of Peter, James and John, He was close to Mary, Martha and Lazarus. Jesus even calls us His friends.

You cannot experience the fullness of God's inspiring life by yourself. You need others in your life. You need friends – people you can trust, be open with and accountable to. Having friends like this is vital to God's unfolding of his purpose in your life. Make a decision today to find a friend. Take the time to share your life with someone. As the days grow darker you will need someone, as Ecclesiastes says, who can, "lift up his companion".

6. Relationships - to Inspire a Community

So far we've talked about living an inspired life which results from knowing Jesus Christ, His purpose, and His plan. It is as we know Him, and are changed to live like Him, that our lives truly become inspiring beyond our families and our relationships will inspire those within our community.

Planted in God's Harvest Field

We serve a sovereign God who has a perfect plan for every person, every neighborhood, every city, and every nation. In His plan, He chooses when and where you will be born. He chooses where He has called you to be assigned to shine as a light in a lost and dark world. One of the most blessed revelations you can receive and know is the fact that God has planted you in His harvest field. Your harvest field is the community in which you live. The Bible says:

> God began by making one person, and from him came all the different people who live everywhere in the world. God decided exactly when and where they must live. Acts 17:26 (NCV)

This means that God is actively working in and through your life to place you where He wants you to inspire others to know Him. He chose you and placed you where you are so that He can shine through you to others. You are planted in God's harvest field. In fact, the Bible shows we are God's field (1 Corinthians 3:9). We are to bring forth the fruit of God's blessing in this field. So, next time you are walking around your neighborhood or work place, know that you are walking in God's field and He is expecting you to plant seeds and see the growth of His Kingdom.

The Greatest News on the Block

Years ago a newspaper boy would ride his bike through the neighborhood and throw the paper early in the morning delivering the latest, greatest news of the previous day. This boy on the bike was the delivery system of the news. Even so, you have news, the greatest news ever to grace this earth. That news is that Jesus Christ came, died, and rose again to impart forgiveness and eternal life to all. In this day of rapid, instant communication it is still the most fantastic, liberating, and blessed news ever to be delivered.

Lt. Col Darrel Cobb

Chris' dad, Lt Col. Darrel Cobb, flew the SR-71 Blackbird during the Vietnam War. It so happened that my dad's best friend, Major Yule, was shot down while flying his B-52 bomber over North Vietnam and he ended up a POW in the Hanoi Hilton.

The day came when the American Military brass wanted to send a signal to the POWs and the personnel of the prison camp that the war was coming to a close. They decided to send up three SR-71s at once and have them all cross over the Hanoi Hilton at the same time. Now, that was no small task since all three of them flew at over Mach 3—faster than a bullet shot from a rifle. When they did, there were multiple sonic booms over the POW camp. It so happened that my dad was one of the three Blackbirds to fly over the prison that day.

So, the story goes that all three were on time, the buildings shook, and the prisoners inside instantly knew there was only one airplane that could make those sounds. The message went out that the booms were the sign that they were going home soon! Later on, Major Yule found out it was his best friend some 80,000 feet above him who was sending him the signal. It was the best news he had heard in a long time.

And so it is within your neighborhood and workplace. You have the good news that many prisoners, people in bondage to sin, need to hear. So, the next time you're out and about in your community, look around and see the potential of God's harvest around you. Many in this field are in bondage to fear, loneliness, drugs, and sin. Most would be open to your praying for them and inviting them to church. You have good news. Share it, give it away and shine in their darkness.

Equipped to Connect With the Lost

One of the results of being connected to Christ is that you can be equipped and empowered by His Holy Spirit. God desires to fill you with His Spirit and equip you so you can reach out and connect others to Him. Not only has God placed you in the "harvest field" and given you the greatest news ever heard, but He will equip you with the gifts, power, and means to see others come to know Him.

The closer you walk with Christ, the more you will want to reflect and shine His message.

For example, look at Jesus' ministry. Jesus effortlessly gave of Himself to share, love, and tell others of the Kingdom of God. He offered forgiveness, hope, and a way of life. He offered an inspired life through His life and message.

Today, it is Jesus Christ working in you to give you the same power, same anointing, and same passion for others that He had. The closer a person walks with Christ, the more they will want to reflect and shine His message to this world. You become His eyes, His feet, and His hands to touch hurting and lost lives. And He equips you to do what He did. Jesus Christ connected people with the Father. When He lives inside you there will be an increasing desire and ability to connect others to God as well. So go take a walk around your block, your workplace and look for those Jesus Christ died for and longs to bring into His Kingdom.

The Priorities for Connected, Inspired Relationships

What holds people together? What drives them apart? How can we build great relationships? Here are five building blocks for great relationships. Do them, and you will succeed.

1. Take a Good Long Look at Yourself

Take a look at yourself before you look around at others who you think may be a "problem" in a relationship. We are often tempted to blame others for broken relationships. Perhaps the real issue is you, not someone else. This is why we are encouraged by Jesus in the Sermon on the Mount (Matthew 5, 6, and 7) to look at ourselves first. The Bible says:

> Hypocrite! First remove the plank from your own eye, and then you will see clearly to remove the speck from your brother's eye. Matthew 7:5

Our nature is to see the faults of others before we see our own. This is a deadly habit and can thin out your friends quickly. Learn to have a positive, encouraging attitude toward others.

2. Commit to Give More Than You Receive

Relax your expectations; let things center more around what you can add rather than what you can get. Enjoy being a blessing without expecting reciprocation and you'll be in Biblical love—never disappointed. This principle is seen in scripture where we are told:

> Whoever refreshes others will be refreshed. Prov. 11:25

So make it an intentional priority to look around and discover who you can bless, encourage, share with, and even listen to. It is the person who gets their eyes off of themselves and focuses on others that is truly living the inspired life. Remember the promise: you refresh others and the Lord will see to it that you are refreshed.

3. Develop Biblical People Skills

Throughout the New Testament there are over fifty-nine "one another" scriptures. These are scripture promises and exhortations that encourage sharing and giving in our relationships. For example consider the following:

Give preference to one another. Romans 12:10

Greet one another with a holy kiss. Romans 16:16

Be kind to one another, tenderhearted. Ephesians 4:32

Open your homes to each other. 1 Peter 4:9

Share each other's troubles. Galatians 6:2

Encourage one another. Hebrews 10:24-25

Did you catch it? Can you see what God wants to say through these and many other references? Just think, what would happen in a home, a family, and in your other relationships if you developed Godly people skills? What would happen if you did as you are told and preferred, greeted, were kind, opened your home, shared, and encouraged one another? Here again is another example of the inspired life being lived out as you reflect in your daily life the people skills of the Lord Jesus Himself.

4. Learn to "Take Out The Trash"

If you have a conflict in a close relationship, reconciliation is vital. Unfinished personal business invites destruction. Some relationships need severing, but most need continual healing. The Bible teaches us that we are to:

> Leave your gift there before the altar, and go your way. First be reconciled to your brother, and then come and offer your gift. Matthew 5:24

We find in this scriptural truth that God is more interested in your healthy relationships than any offering you may bring Him. It's like God is saying, "Go take care of your personal issues before you come see Me." Thus, if you have offended, spoke harshly, wronged, rejected, and even got upset at another person, you need to first "take out the trash" of your heart before you go see the Master.

> *"Go take care of your personal issues before you come see Me."*

He's more interested in your heart being right than any offering you can bring Him. Keep your heart sincere and clean before Him and then bring your offering. If your family or local church were to do this on a consistent basis, then you would be assured of God's commanded blessing in your presence.

In Summary

The best gifts in life that God gives us come wrapped in relationships. But relationships take effort. You have to work at them, keeping Biblical truths in mind. The world gives us the wrong message: put yourself first; it's all about you. But God's Word shows us a better way: take a look at yourself, make time, commit to give, get some skills, and take out the trash.

In this chapter we discussed five levels of connection a believer will walk in resulting from his or her relationship with Jesus Christ. First you are vitally connected to Jesus Christ because He lives in you. Then we discussed the blessing of belonging to His family, the church. We touched on the benefit and God's plan when you are connected in marriage. We talked about growing a connected family. Lastly, you shine as a light when you are connected to your harvest field, the place where God planted you to bring forth fruit on this earth.

No person can be a follower of Christ by themselves. Make a choice to no longer live alone. God desires to connect you with others. He wants them to be a blessing to you and you to them. God placed you together with others to enjoy life, His life, yes, even His inspired life.

Chapter 5

Shining in the Darkness: The Power of Your Influence

You are the light of the world. A city that is set on a hill cannot be hidden. Matthew 5:14

Let your light so shine before men, that they may see your good works and glorify your Father in heaven. Matthew 5:16

Do you realize the opportunity of a lifetime is within your reach? Yes, you have right in front of you the power to change the course of history. You have the privilege and potential to offer others around you something that is life changing and powerful. And that is the power of eternal life with God.

You see, the inspired life is a life of supernatural influence. Stop and think about that for a moment. There is nothing this world offers that comes close to the inspired life you can give away to others because of your relationship with Jesus Christ. You can literally step out of your front door today, walk out into this world, and offer the most powerful solution to mankind's needs ever known.

You can pray with someone, see them come to know Christ, see their body healed, their heart filled with hope and encouragement, and their fears dispelled. With one simple prayer you can see years of pain, sin, guilt, and shame washed away through God's love and forgiveness. You can see a life of hopelessness, despair, loneliness, and sorrow picked up and started all over again. You can be the answer to someone's cry for help. You can rescue a soul from eternal darkness. Yes, today you can make the difference in someone's life. You can be an inspiring influence that will change someone's life forever!

You can be an inspired life changing agent.

Let's start this section with a restatement of what it means to inspire others. For the sake of this chapter we are defining "inspiring influence" as:

A person of influence who has the capacity, ability, and power to be an inspiration, encouragement, and motivation on the actions, behavior, opinions, etc., of others.

This can be you. You have the capacity and ability in God to be an inspiration to others. You have the power to encourage and motivate others actions, behaviors, and opinions. You can do this! Now's let's find out how.

It's Time to Turn on the Lights

Jesus Christ started His ministry in Galilee. We are told the conditions of this region in His day was one of darkness. We read in Matthew's gospel that the people "sat in the region and shadow of death." (Matthew 4:16). And it was in this darkness we are told these people "saw a great light." Let's read the full text of scripture where we learn:

Jesus Stepped Into the Darkness of People's Lives

The people who sat in darkness have seen a great light. And upon those who sat in the region and shadow of death light has dawned. Matthew 4:15-16

It was in this dark region that Jesus Christ began to turn on the lights. He intentionally and deliberately entered into this region to light a flame. Most religious leaders would have started in Jerusalem, the hub of religious activity in that day. Surely, this is where the good news of God's love would start, right? But not Jesus. No, His ministry was no typical religious activity of the day. He had a new message: the hope of the Messiah, and the dreams of a new kingdom. He went to the greatest needs first: those sitting under the shadow of darkness.

> *Jesus went to the greatest needs first: those sitting under the shadow of darkness.*

It was in this darkness that Jesus Christ said, "I am the light of the world" (John 8:12). And shine He did. Jesus entered this region and began to inspire people with His presence like no one had ever done before. His words, His manners, His deeds, His miracles, and His presence dispelled darkness, challenged demon strongholds, and ushered in a whole new way of living—Kingdom living. Yes, it was Jesus offering His people the opportunity and means to come out of years of darkness and bondage.

It was the message of His Father that the Kingdom of Heaven was now here and available, with all its power, presence, and glory. It was the fulfillment of all that the prophets had spoken regarding God promises. And then Jesus made one of the most astounding statements ever heard by mankind:

Jesus Commissioned You to Shine

You are the light of the world. Matthew 5:14

Incredible! He was talking to sinners! He was talking to common everyday folk who were sick, lived with hang ups, sinful habits, anger, and religious unbelief. They may have been alcoholics, maybe a few prostitutes, and, oh my, He told them they are the light of the world! Really? Yes, it was to these people Jesus came with the express purpose of offering them a way out of darkness and into an inspired, fulfilled, and purposeful life. He offered them the Kingdom of God.

John Wesley

John Wesley, founder of the Methodist Church, was often challenged by the Anglican Church because of his disregard of church order and protocol. They wanted him to preach "in the church." It was in the church building where ministry was to take place. But John ventured out into public and had the audacity to preach Christ to the common folk, the sinners, and those not going to church. He preached in the open air. Oh my, John was actually preaching in the marketplace, the parks, without pews, pulpits, and the proper robes of the clergy. When the Anglican Church demanded that John preach inside the church he replied, "Why preach in the church? I need to go where the people are…and they are out there…not in the church.

Jesus went on to encourage people by saying:

Let your light so shine before men, that they may see your good works and glorify your Father in heaven. Matthew 5:16

Jesus was encouraging His people to shine and He wanted others to see the light. This light that Jesus brought was not to be hidden away. No, Jesus Christ turned on the high beams and told His people to do the same. He wanted those around to see His people shining with the influence of an inspired life. A life touched by the Master, lifted by His love, and propelled into His purpose. Jesus said, "a city set on a hill cannot be hidden. You can't light a lamp and put it under a basket. No, you put the lamp on a lampstand and it gives light to all" (Matthew 5:14).

The Graveyard of the Atlantic

Off the shore of North Carolina, near the outer banks of the continental shelf, lies one of the worst stretches of ocean in the world. Over the past 400 years, over 300 ships have sunk in this small area. It's called "The Graveyard of the Atlantic" because of a fourteen mile sandbar called the "Diamond Shoals." Seeing the need to warn ships of the danger, the U.S. government built a lighthouse on Cape Hatteras in 1870. The Cape Hatteras Lighthouse is the largest in the United States, roughly twelve stories high with forty-eight inch thick walls. What is the main purpose of that lighthouse? It was built to warn ships and save those at risk of being lost at sea.

When you think about it, the church's mission is the same as that lighthouse. Our world is a dark and dangerous place. People are sailing rough seas and the devil is committed to sinking anyone who gives him a chance. We see the wreckage every day. But Jesus calls the church to get involved. Instead of just watching the damage, He calls us to shine; to be an influence in the lives of others.

I love to picture the church as a lighthouse. Light shines and shows the way. If we fail to shine people perish, but if we shine like He said people are rescued and made safe. Are you saved?

Engaging the Darkness

Influence can also be understood as "the power to sway or affect."[12] Who are we to influence?

Our Neighbors

Love your neighbor as yourself. There is no greater commandment... Mark 12:31

There is a world in danger all around us. At work, on campus, in our family, and right here in the church people are in danger. Influence begins right where you are. Jesus taught us to love our neighbors. So, do you know your neighbors? Do you have any level of relationship with them?

In today's society, especially here in the Bay Area, it is sometimes difficult to even meet our neighbors. But the principle remains, we're to love our neighbors. And sometimes this love means stepping out of our comfort zone and into the lives of

---

[12] Dictionary.com, "*Influence*" 2015 Dictionary.com LLC http://dictionary.reference.com/browse/influence?s=t

those around us. Which means we pray and believe God for an open door to reach out to our neighbors with the intent of establishing some type of relationship.

For the past several years Chris and his wife Carol passed out cookies to the neighbors on our block during Christmas. They include a Christmas Card, a short prayer, and who they are. Just doing this simple act has opened the door to meet more people on our block. What about you? Who are your neighbors and what can you do to reach out to them, get to know them, find a need they have, and eventually find the opportunity to pray with them?

The Needy and Less Fortunate

We must identify with the hurts that are around us and be willing to help others who hurt. Just think about how Jesus influenced you in your time of need. Can you do less?

> [The righteous] share freely and give generously to those in need. Their good deeds will be remembered forever. They will have influence and honor. Psalms 112:9 (NLT)

Every day there are people in pain all around us. People are in the hospital. Some people are going through marriage challenges. Many have fears, worries, financial lack, mental oppression, anxiety, and so forth.

One of the greatest opportunities to live an inspired life of influence is to simply look for those in need and offer to pray for them.

Make it a priority in your life to look for those in need. Allow the compassion of the Lord to lead you to help them. You never know who the Holy Spirit will lead you to. Be open and available to God and choose to influence those in need with an open hand of His grace and His love.

The Influencers in Our Community

Within any community there are those individuals who are the major influencers. For example, there are political figures, educational professionals, sport personalities, and other prominent professionals such as CEOs, radio or TV personalities, etc. Even though these people are the influencers in the community, the question is "who is going to influence them?"

Many times God will use pastors or regular church folk to engage with the top influencers of a community for the express purpose of sharing Christ, praying for their needs, and leading them to salvation. We have found that even high profile personalities have just as much need and desire to know God as anyone else. They just need to find people they can relate to, trust, and share their hearts with. The Bible tells us:

> Do you see someone skilled in their work? They will serve before kings. Proverbs 22:29

Yes, God desires to find faithful influencers who will, in turn, stand before the influencers of a community. Again, pray for those who have influence in your community. Be open to the leading of the Lord and watch who God will bring your way through the course of your everyday life.

The Workforce

One of the greatest opportunities to be a person of influence is your place of employment. God places you in a job, a company, and a location so that you can shine as a light and engage with those you work with.

In fact, to be a person of influence in your workplace you first need to see that your primary responsibility is to bring God's light into the workplace, and what you do for employment is secondary.

Let's say you work in a bank, a high-tech marketing company, or a retail store. Each of these are really launching points for God to use you to influence those around you with His grace and love. You may be working at the bank and God will bring people to you every day who may have a need in their life. Your first responsibility is to those God brings you and to look for the opportunity to share Christ.

God is moving in the work place like never before in history. Believers are learning that they have a calling and an anointing to step into the darkness of a company and bring the influence of the Kingdom. Quite often believers will share, pray with a co-worker, or start a Bible study at the workplace. Other co-workers will see, hear, and ask questions.

You have a calling and an anointing to step into the darkness of a company and bring the influence of the Kingdom.

As you are faithful, God will empower you to influence those around you and equip you to be a light in the darkness. Make a decision today to bring light into your workplace. Pray for the people around you. Look for opportunities to offer prayer and help to others. And as you pray, God will open the door for you to be an influencer for His Kingdom.

The Christian Receptionist

Years ago we heard of a church member who started a new job as a receptionist for a local company. She brought her Bible to work and read it during lunch. She quickly found out in the first week there were five other women at the company who were openly anti-Christ and promoted witchcraft. They immediately began to ridicule, mock, and challenge the new Christian employee.

Well, this Christian lady went home after the first week and cried out to God and asked why He had allowed her to get the job in such a dark setting with ungodly people. She heard the Holy Spirit tell her that God put her in that place to shine for Him. That one word gave her the courage to not back down, but engage the darkness with the love and kindness of the Lord. After several months of continuing to love in the face of harsh mockery, she eventually led two of the witches to the Lord and the other three either quit or were fired. Now that's living God's inspired life and engaging the darkness, even in the workplace.

The Next Generation

God wants the generational light to keep shining. God's light is not just for us, and we can't let the light go out in the next generation. We must pass the torch on. In fact, this is God's plan. He wants the firm commitment of His people to pass on His anointing and commission to the next generation.

For over 2,000 years there has been an unbroken link of God's salvation shining on this earth. There have been dark years where the light of His gospel looked like it was going out. But nevertheless, Jesus said He'll build His church and He will see to it that the next generation will hear of His goodness. The Bible says:

> He commanded our ancestors to teach [His laws] to their children, so the next generation might know them—even the children not yet born—and they in turn will teach their own children. Psalms 78:5-6 (NLT)

Did you notice the phrase, "even the children not yet born"? Friends, God is looking for His people to live such an inspired life that even the generations to come will hear of our legacy, faithfulness, and influence. You are to influence your generations to come. The Bible says:

> A good person leaves an inheritance for their children's children. Proverbs 13:22

If you have children, are you planning on leaving an inheritance to their children? If you are single, or don't have children, you can certainly find members of the younger generation whom you can influence. You can impart, mentor, and love with the influence of Christ.

Make it your aim in life to not only live for yourself, but to live for the generations to come.

Make it your aim in life to not only live for yourself, but to live for the generations to come. Make it a goal to leave a legacy of your inspired life down through the generations. There are many younger men and women in your community who are looking for someone to help them, guide, them, love and lead them into their purpose in life. If you take the time you can leave a legacy in their lives.

Look for "The One"

When we speak of shining in the darkness and influencing the world for Christ, it is vital that you capture the heart and the passion the Lord has for the lost. Throughout scripture, as you walk with Christ, you will find that Jesus Christ has a never ending well of compassion and zeal for people.

As pastors, we are concerned and we need to be careful that people don't become another statistic or data point in our ministry. But as believers, when we look at Jesus we quickly find a burning desire in Him for the lost, the wounded, and the hurting.

Take, for example, Jesus' discussion with the religious leaders found in Luke's gospel, chapter 15. In this passage of scripture, we find three parables back to back on the same subject. This is the only place in scripture where Jesus does this. Obviously, this should impress upon us the importance of the topic. The three parables, in summary, deal with a lost sheep, a woman who lost a coin, and a man who was the father of a prodigal son.

These parables are included in this section because we need to understand the way the Lord lays out these parables. For it is in these parables we find three distinct characteristics: something or someone was lost, a search was made, and a celebration took place after that which was lost was found. Let's take a look at each of these specific lessons.

Something Was Lost

Jesus said a man had one hundred sheep and "one" went astray. Many would have been happy with just keeping the ninety-nine. "Oh well," some may say, "we still have the ninety-nine." But not the shepherd. No, he noticed that a sheep was missing. And that one sheep was important to him!

Then Jesus spoke of a woman who had ten coins. She took notice that something was missing: one of her coins.

Then there was the father of the prodigal son. He, too, knew his son was gone; missing. And it was the father that looked, perhaps daily, for the son's return.

Friends, do you know someone who perhaps served the Lord for a while and is not in fellowship? Is there a family member who is separated from others? Or, perhaps there was a new member in your small group Bible study that came for a few weeks and then disappeared?

A person living an inspired life is called to look for "one" who is lost.

Jesus Christ is concerned about the "one"; that is His mission. Are we as concerned about the "one" as Christ is? A person living an inspired life is called to influence others and even look out for that which is lost. Stop and think about those around you who perhaps are no longer connected. Then plan to take action to do something about it.

The Search Is On

We're told that the shepherd "went after that one which is lost" (Luke 15:4). The woman who lost her coin "lit a lamp, swept the house, and searched carefully until she found it" (Luke 15:8). The father probably looked daily for the son to come home. There was a hope, an expectation, and a yearning for his lost son (Luke 15:20).

When was the last time you sought after that one person who was lost, in need, and looking for help? Today we have mobile phones, email, texting, and all sorts of technology to help us search and connect with those who are lost. Stop and think about friends, relatives, or others you know who at one time served the Lord, or expressed an interest in Church. Where are they today? If they are not present, let the search begin. Go find them. Share Christ's love with them. Bring them back. Believe God for restoration and a return to His goodness. It all starts with recognizing something is lost and then you make an effort to start the search.

Celebration Time

Notice in all three parables that once that which was lost was found, there was a tremendous celebration that took place. Jesus said when the sheep was found that the shepherd called his neighbors to rejoice with him. Likewise the woman when she found her coin. And the father held a party when his son had returned home.

Jesus says, "there will be more joy in heaven over one sinner who repents" (Luke 15:7). Wow! Joy in heaven! Yes, the angels rejoice, and the celebration begins. Why? Because Jesus was teaching us the value of a soul and the celebration that occurs because one more person has received Him as Lord. Let us not take for granted or minimize the importance over the "one" sheep, or the "one" coin, or the "one" son who returns. Jesus is very concerned about the "one." Jesus gave His life for that "one" who was lost and is now found.

In order to live a life of influence don't minimize the impact you have on one person. Today, you have an opportunity to search for the "one" and celebrate when they return. Make a decision today to influence "one" person. Be a blessing to "one" person. Look for and bring back that "one" person. And then let the party begin when that which is lost is found!

Taking Care of the Harvest

Chris grew up down the street from a cotton field in southwest Oklahoma. Every year the farmer would plow the field and plant cotton. In the latter part of the summer he would harvest the cotton. This farmer planted the seed with the intent to reap a harvest. And the farmer likewise expected the harvest to be profitable.

In the church, however, many times a "harvest" of souls is forgotten, overlooked, or left out in the field. Sometimes there is no intentional plan to keep and care for the "harvest." This is why it is vital that the members of a local church have a specific plan to care for new believers. A plan to help them get grounded and begin growing in Christ.

To be a person, or church, of influence you must take the time and necessary steps to care for new believers. They need to be prayed with, visited, and brought into a vital relationship with the Lord and the local church. It's not enough to say you are a person of influence unless you take responsibility for following through and ensuring those you touch have an opportunity to continue their relationship with the Lord.

John the Apostle

Eusebius Pamphili, an early church historian and Bishop of Caesarea in the year 314 wrote of the Apostle John and his ministry when he came back to Asia Minor after being exiled to Patmos. Eusebius notes it was during this exile that the Lord appeared to John and gave direction to write the seven letters found in the book of Revelation to the churches of Asia Minor. We're told John got off the island and delivered the letters.

Afterward John went out again, now in his 90's, and continued planting churches. He came to one area, planted a church, set up the leadership, and also led a young man to the Lord who previously was a thief and had led a band of robbers. He committed the young man to the pastor of the new church and told him to "disciple the one who God committed to their trust." John left, continued his ministry, and after some time came back to the church. After discussing church matters, John asked about the young man and his status. The pastor told John that the young man had left the faith and was back leading his band of thieves in the mountains.

Eusebius notes that John turned on the spot and went up into the hills after the young man. The story goes that John was met by the gang members who proceeded to assault him. But off in the distance John saw the young man he had led to the Lord and he cried out, "Come back to the one who loved you." John followed the young man, knelt before him, kissed his hand, and pleaded with him to come back to Christ. The young man broke, repented, and gave his heart back to the Lord. John then brought him back to the church and back to the pastor who was to care for his soul. And again, John impressed upon the pastor the need to care for the one who was committed to his trust.

We tell this story because there is a harvest of souls coming into the Kingdom of God every day around the world. And God is looking for those whom He can trust to care for the new souls. It would do little good if we live an inspired life and influence others but we don't have the capacity or passion to care for and disciple those whom God has entrusted us with.

Can the Lord trust you to care for one of His? Just as parents bring a new child into the world and spend the necessary time and resources to care for that child, even so the church needs to care for those coming in through our influence. It takes time. It takes effort.

Sometimes there are sleepless nights and endless hours carrying the baby in the hallways at 3:00 a.m. in the morning. But it is all worth it to the parent as they watch their child grow. Even so, it is worth it as we live the inspired life of Christ, influence the world, and see new believers come to Christ and begin to grow and reflect His goodness and grace.

Reproducing Christ—the First Days of a New Believer

The purpose of this section is to impress upon you the importance of the first few days, weeks, and months of a new believer. All too often people make a commitment to follow the Lord and then are left on their own to figure out what the

Christian life is and what all it means.

The First Days of a New Believer

Many times men and women will receive Christ and then not fully understand what just took place. We in the church many times take for granted that a simple prayer is made and someone is born again. But often the one saying the prayer is not even aware of the words, the phrases spoken, and the depth of what it means to be a Christian.

It is vital that the new believers be contacted, visited, and encouraged in their decision to follow Christ.

The days immediately following a new believer's choice can make all the difference between continuing to grow in Christ or forsaking Christ and turning back to the world. It is important that the new believer be contacted, visited, and encouraged in their decision to follow Christ. It is important to pray for them, and with them, again.

Many times new believers have immediate needs in their life that we can help them with. Some need guidance regarding family matters. Many need help understanding who Jesus is and why they needed to be born again. Regardless of the need, suffice it say that someone needs to connect with the new believer and take responsibility for their growth in Christ. We need to follow up and ensure they get connected to a small group Bible study and a local church. They need a friend they can call and someone who will take a real interest in their life.

The Battle For the Soul

Jesus Christ gave us the parable about a farmer sowing seed in the ground, yet some of the seed fell by the wayside. In this parable, Jesus gives us insight to the spiritual warfare that ensues when a person hears God's word and turns to Him. Jesus said:

> ...these are the ones by the wayside where the word is sown. When they hear, Satan comes immediately and takes away the word that was sown in their hearts. Mark 4:15

Notice Jesus said, "Satan comes immediately"! This is why the first few hours, and days, of a new believer's soul are in the balance. Once they receive Christ, a battle is engaged and a war is waged upon them to take away that which God has planted in their heart. We need to remember this and understand that the person who receives Christ has just entered the battle zone. We need to be there to help, pray, intercede, and protect that new believer from the onslaught of doubt, discouragement, or anything else that would deter their faith in Christ.

Until Christ is Formed in You

The Apostle Paul lived an inspired life and, through his letters in the New Testament, continues to influence believers around the world. In his writing to the various churches, we find the passion of a man who cared for new souls and carefully took the time to ensure that the harvest God gave him would grow and stay strong. But one time, Paul encountered a group of believers in the area of Galatia who began to drift from the faith that he had imparted to them. This became such a burden to Paul that in his letter to the Galatians he said:

> My little children, over whom I travail in birth again until Christ be formed in you... Galatians 4:19

Paul's goal for the church in Galatia was that Christ be formed in them. This desire and passion was so strong that Paul equated it to a woman travailing while giving birth to a child. Now that's what we call an intense passion!

A woman giving birth experiences a lot of pressure, pushing, expanding of the cervical muscles, and continual contractions until the child is born. Chris and his wife Carol have six kids; Chris saw his wife birth all six. And he witness his faithful, loving wife spend a lot of energy, pain, and pressure to birth those kids. On her birthday and Mother's day the kids continually thank her and ask her forgiveness for putting her through such an ordeal.

So it is in the spiritual realm. Paul labored, pushed, sweated, and travailed in prayer for the people of Galatia. Have you ever felt this way for new believers? Have you exerted yourself, your time, and your energy to travail for someone in Christ until they are grounded and birthed in God? Sometimes this is necessary. But the question is, are you ready for God to use you to this extent as you grow into a person of influence?

Practical Strategies to Influence Your Community

Here are some practical steps you can take to step into the inspired life; a life of influencing others for Christ. Read carefully and discover what strategies you can begin living out.

Individually

Write down the names of those you know who don't know Jesus Christ. This list could include close family members, relatives, neighbors, or co-workers. Ask the Lord to remind you and lead you as you make this list. It is this list that you will begin with to start living a life of influence.

After you have created the list, begin to set aside time to pray for them on a regular basis. Include them in your daily prayer time. It is as you pray that the Holy Spirit will begin to work in their lives and open their hearts to know Him. And He will prepare their hearts and make a way so that you can share with them.

Next, you'll want to contact those individuals. Many people call just to say "hello." Some connect with them to take them out for coffee or a meal. Quite often we encourage other types of connection points such as a BBQ, a movie, beach party, or some other activity that these individuals can be invited to. It is during these times of connection that God will open the doors for you to share. There are many stories of friends and family coming to know the Lord because they were identified, prayed for, and invited to a "connection" event. You can do this, too, and you will be surprised what God will do.

Influence Through Your Small Groups of Believers

Not only can you influence friends for Christ on an individual basis, but also collectively in a small group. A small group Bible study is the perfect setting for a group of believers. In a safe environment, you can share with the group your friends and relatives who don't know Christ and everyone can pray for them. Then, as a group, you can come up with a variety of plans for connecting and inviting those unsaved people. A great motivator for people to gather is always food. Many groups simply have a picnic at a park. Some host a BBQ where all of the group is encouraged to bring their friends.

Again, the ideas for connecting people are limitless. The important concept to grasp is the power of a group identifying, praying, and connecting with those who don't know Christ. Thus the power of your influence is magnified and together you can reach out and demonstrate the inspired life.

Engaging Your Community Church Wide

Many churches combine the power of small groups and influence whole communities for the cause of Christ. This is extremely powerful because it doesn't take a lot of resources to make a big difference within the region you live.

We suggest that churches plan on reaching out to communities in and through small groups. When a small group is intent on impacting a region not only will they see people come to Christ, but they can also establish new territory for Christ as the new believers are discipled and more small groups are planted. Using these strategies many churches plant new churches, establish multi-site communities, and intentionally spread their influence by moving into an area and then staying there.

Robert Belair

Robert Belair, at the Institute for Advanced Study at Princeton University says, "We shouldn't underestimate the significance of the small group of people who have a vision of a just and gentle world. The quality of a whole culture may be changed when two percent of its people have a new vision."[13]

In Summary

God has called every believer to live an inspired life to influence this world. This call includes you. As you live out God's inspired life, knowing Jesus Christ, you will desire to influence and touch other's lives as well. This desire is a natural response to Christ's inspired life overflowing through you to a lost world.

Today, ask God to fill you and direct your steps to live out a life of influence to those around you. Pray for the passion and power to share, give, and gather the harvest of souls into God's Kingdom. Other than knowing Jesus Christ there is no greater fulfillment in life than to see other's lives changed and brought into His Kingdom.

Today, let your light shine. Make a difference in another person's life. Be a person of influence as you go your way. Allow your eyes to be used by God to see the potential of what He can do in this world.

---

[13] Christianity Today, *"Four Ways Christians Can Influence the World"*, John Stott, October, 2011

http://www.christianitytoday.com/ct/2011/october/saltlight.html?start=5

Chapter 6

God's Rewards for You!

Imagine with us for a few minutes that you are standing in line with the millions of other believers on that great and awesome day of the Lord. The day and time when all of God's people are together as one before Jesus Christ our Lord and Savior. Everyone is there: King David, Moses, Deborah of the Judges, and the prophets of old such as Isaiah and Daniel. Then there is Peter, John, and Mary and Martha. Then you spot your relatives who've gone on before you. Your grandpa, your kids, friends, and so on. Everyone who throughout time received Jesus Christ as Lord will be there. It will be a glorious day! This is the day of the marriage supper of the Lamb spoken of in Revelation 19:7:

> Let us rejoice and exult and give him the glory, for the marriage of the Lamb has come, and his Bride has made herself ready.

And then your name is called over the loud speaker in Heaven! Everyone begins to cheer! The angels stand and rejoice. The multitudes of the saints see you escorted before the Lord and everyone is clapping and giving high-fives. There is Jesus, smiling and welcoming you to stand on the stage with Him before all His people. And then... you hear His voice reverberate before the crowd as He proclaims over you:

> Well done, good and faithful servant! Come and share your master's happiness! Matthew 25:23 (NIV)

Everyone cheers and there is an eruption of praise to the Lamb for what He's done for you. And then... drum roll please... Jesus announces your name before His Father. Remember, Jesus says:

> Whoever acknowledges me before others, I will also acknowledge before my Father in heaven. Matthew 10:32 (NIV)

Now Jesus turns to the section reserved for His angels. Michael the archangel, and Gabriel, will be there along with the host of all the other angels. Jesus says:

> I tell you, whoever publicly acknowledges me before others, the Son of Man will also acknowledge before the angels of God. Luke 12:8 (NIV)

Now comes the best part of the awards ceremony. The time when Jesus acknowledges you for overcoming the world, trusting in Him as your savior, and walking with Him on this earth as one of His. Yes, there are going to be millions of believers whom the Lord desires to announce before the Father and the angels. Millions will hear the words "well done!"

But then there is bestowed upon you honor and grace for fighting the battles, standing strong against sin and unrighteousness, and trying your best to live an inspired life while you were on this earth. Jesus Christ made an astounding statement while on this earth. He said;

> If anyone serves me, the Father will honor him. John 12:26

Wow! Receiving the honor of the Father! The original Greek language here speaks of "esteeming highly and placing great value and worth upon someone."[14] Further, it means to "hold someone as special and to show endearing love and honor." We have an example of this when Jesus was baptized by John in the river Jordan. When Jesus came out of the water a voice was heard from Heaven:

> This is my beloved Son, with whom I am well pleased. Matthew 3:17

Could it be that you, too, will hear those words? Will God say of you, *"This is my beloved son or daughter, in whom I am well pleased"*? Yes, there will be a time of honor, blessings, and rewards for you, along with the multitudes of saints gone before you. We will all worship and celebrate the Lord and He in turn will open up an endless stream of His grace and kindness the likes of which we've never experienced before. The Bible says,

> Now God has us where he wants us, with all the time in this world and the next to shower grace and kindness upon us in Christ Jesus. Ephesians 2:7 (MSG)

Yes, forever we'll be with Him and receive His grace, as well as His honor, upon us. He will continually be celebrating His creation as we in turn worship Him as Lord of all. It's going to be an awesome time in Heaven, friends!

---

[14] Blueletter Bible, quoting Strong's Concordance, Number G5091
http://www.blueletterbible.org/lang/lexicon/lexicon.cfm?Strongs=G5091&t=KJV

10 Christ-Like Characteristics of Those God Rewards

God loves to reward and bless His people. The following list of twelve characteristics of rewards shows us God's heart, how He rewards, and the conditions which God sees as noteworthy to reward.

1. Rewards for a Giving Heart

When you do a charitable deed, do not let your left hand know what your right hand is doing, that your charitable deed may be in secret; and your Father who sees in secret will Himself reward you openly. Matthew 6:4

There are rewards for those who give. Notice Jesus said the Father sees your giving to the poor and hurting and He desires to reward you. The principle is simple. God is looking to reward His people for sharing and giving to others and He is watching. So, go ahead, give generously and do a good deed today. You'll be rewarded for it.

2. Rewards for the Prayer Warrior

When you pray, go into your room, and when you have shut your door, pray to your Father who is in the secret place; and your Father who sees in secret will reward you openly. Matthew 6:6

God rewards the prayer warriors. Others may not see you praying by yourself, in the quiet of night, as you are alone worshipping and praying to Him. But God is looking to reward those who call out to Him with a clean and pure heart. So, go ahead and pray in secret today, and know this, you have an audience of One who desires to reward you.

3. Rewards to Those Who Fast

When you fast, anoint your head and wash your face, so that you do not appear to men to be fasting, but to your Father who is in the secret place; and your Father who sees in secret will reward you openly." Matthew 6:18

Fasting is a spiritual discipline you choose in order to separate yourself from the daily activities of meals and business in order to more effectively seek God. Jesus said the Father likewise is looking for His people to fast and He desires to reward you for it. When you fast, know this, whatever is on your heart as to the reason for the fast, God sees and He desires to work on your behalf. So, sometime soon, set aside a day to fast and commit it to the Lord. Then get ready, as God will work on your behalf.

4. Rewards for a Life of Purity

The Lord rewarded me according to my righteousness and according to the cleanness of my hands He has recompensed me. Psalms 18:20

God is looking to reward and bless those who live upright before Him. With all the ungodliness and defilement in our culture today, it is rare to find those who desire to stay clean in heart before God. But as you pursue the Lord, and desire to live pure before Him, know this, there is the reward of His presence, joy, and blessing that no one can take away. So, is it worth it to stay clean before God? You bet!

5. Rewards for Keeping God's Word

Moreover by them Your servant is warned, And in keeping them there is great reward. Psalms 19:11

There is a great reward for those who keep, obey, and live out God's word in their lives. The rewards of obeying God's word are the promises of God found in His word. You will be rewarded and blessed as you read, meditate, and live out God's truth in your life.

6. Rewards for Doing Good

But he who sows righteousness will have a sure reward. Proverbs 11:18

God is looking to reward those who do good, live right, give to the poor, and stand for righteousness. It is not politically correct in many circles of life today to "sow righteousness." There are major forces in the world today that seek to pervert what is right and they will challenge you when you stand up for truth. But God sees when you sow what is right into this world and it will not go unnoticed. You will be rewarded.

7. Rewards for Blessing Your Enemy

If your enemy is hungry, give him bread to eat...and the LORD will reward you. Proverbs 25:21-22

When you give to and love your enemy, you are sharing the heart of God's love for this world. The Lord sees this and He notices those who love as He loves. He then rewards those who live out their lives as a lover of people, especially when they love their enemies.

8. Rewards for Giving a Cup of Water

And whoever gives one of these little ones only a cup of cold water in the name of a disciple, assuredly, I say to you, he shall by no means lose his reward. Matthew 10:42

Is there a reward for giving a cup of water? Sure! The principle here is that God notices even the little things we do in life when we bless others. This tells us God delights in rewarding and blessing those who give even in the small things. So, go fill a cup with water and give it away today. God will see it and bless you for it.

9. Rewards for Holding Fast to Your Faith

Therefore do not cast away your confidence, which has great reward. Hebrews 10:35

Jesus Christ is looking to reward those who hold fast, stand firm, and overcome life's challenges. Everyday we must make choices to stand strong in God's truth. God sees those who are persevering and holding fast to His promises and He promises to reward them.

10. Rewards According to Your Work

I am coming quickly, and My reward is with Me, to give to every one according to his work. Revelation 22:12

Most Christians know Jesus Christ is coming back again to this earth and everyone will see Him. But did you know He's coming with rewards? Yes, Jesus will give rewards to those who keep His word, obey, and live faithfully before Him on this earth. So when He returns, are you expecting Jesus to be a God of judgment or a God who rewards you? If you live for Him and stay true, you'll be blessed to know that He's coming for you and He will be rewarding you. So, again, is it worth it to stay true and walk with Him? Yes—believe it!

God's Rewards and Honor for You in Heaven

The following scriptures share God's heart in desiring to honor and bless you. As you walk with Him and live out an inspiring life, there will be a day when you will be celebrated!

1. You're invited to Heaven's wedding celebration

"Let us rejoice and exult and give him the glory, for the marriage of the Lamb has come, and his Bride has made herself ready." Revelations 19:7

There is coming a time when the church will be joined together with the Lord Jesus. It is during this time you will join in the celebration where Jesus will honor His bride.

2. Jesus Announces Your Name to the Father

"Therefore whoever confesses Me before men, him I will also confess before My Father who is in heaven." Matthew 10:32

Yes, Jesus Himself will make an announcement of your name personally before your Father in Heaven.

3. Jesus Introduces You to His Angels

"I tell you, whoever publicly acknowledges me before others, the Son of Man will also acknowledge before the angels of God." Luke 12:8 (NIV)

Next Jesus will declare introduce you before His angels.

4. Jesus Rewards your Faithfulness

'Well done, good and faithful servant; you have been faithful over a few things, I will make you ruler over many things. Enter into the joy of your lord.
Matthew 25:23

When your name is called out in Heaven all of God's creation will rejoice and celebrate you for a job well done. God will reward you for your faithfulness with promotions to new levels of responsibility in Heaven.

We are going to review two general areas in the remainder of this chapter with respect to the Lord's rewards. We'll first review twelve different characteristics of the lives that the Lord sees and desires to reward. We'll then discover the purpose of God in rewarding His promises to us today, *before* we arrive in Heaven.

God desires to continually and abundantly bless His us out of His love for us.

There is a reason we want to draw your attention to God's rewards. As we walk with Him, and make the decision to live an inspired life, God desires to show before all creation the fact that there were people who, while in a sinful world, decided to follow Him, love Him, and trust Him for the work accomplished on the cross. All too often believers go through their Christian lives living well below God's promises and blessings. They fail to realize that God desires to bless them, and that He wants to reward them for following Him.

The greatest gift we receive from Him is that of eternal life and the forgiveness of our sins. But that is just the starting point and entry into the life of God. He desires to continually and abundantly bless His people out of His love for us.

Let's start with specific characteristics of a life that God rewards. As you read though this list take note that God says He wants to reward you. Many shy away and count themselves unworthy of His love and rewards. Don't let that false humility shroud your life and limit His blessing. No, as you find your purpose in God, take the time to praise Him and thank Him for His rewards and blessings in your life.

God's Rewards and His Promises Today

The Bible tells us that the Lord Jesus takes great pleasure in rewarding, blessing, and bringing joy to His people. Someone once counted and found that there are 7,487 promises in the Bible which overwhelmingly display God's pleasure and joy as He lavishes His love upon us. The Bible tells us:

> God has us where he wants us, with all the time in this world and the next to shower grace and kindness upon us

in Christ Jesus. Ephesians 2:7 (MSG)

For eternity without end, the Lord Jesus will continue to unfold the magnificence of His glory and forever we'll be in amazement and awe of who He is. The Bible also tells us that:

He is a rewarder of those who diligently seek Him. Hebrews 11:6

Yes, for those who seek Him diligently, the Lord desires to reward them. This principle is seen throughout the Bible in various ways and examples. But all too often many Christians believe they have to wait until they are in Heaven before they can start to receive His rewards. This is partially true in that there are many promises which God has reserved for you in eternity. But there are also many rewards available to you now, today, on this side of Heaven. The Bible tells us:

Blessed be the God and Father of our Lord Jesus Christ, who has blessed us with every spiritual blessing in the heavenly places in Christ. Ephesians 1:3

Notice the phrase surrounding God's blessing is in the past tense. This tells us that His provision for blessing is already available to us today. There are many, many promises the Lord desires to reward us with in the here and now and we don't have to wait for eternity to enjoy them. For example, God promises us salvation and eternity with Him. He promises us His peace, joy, healing, leading, guiding, strength, power, and authority. Just read through the Bible and take a Bible marking pencil and circle or underline all of God's promises and you'll find that a large majority are already waiting for you to claim and receive as God's reward today.

God's Reward is God Himself

The reason we want to emphasize this principle is because behind God's rewards and blessings is the truth that when we receive of God's rewards we are really receiving an extension of Himself. The Bible tells us:

> His divine power has given to us all things that pertain to life and godliness, ...by which have been given to us exceedingly great and precious promises, that through these you may be partakers of the divine nature. 2 Peter 1:3-4

This little passage of scripture is loaded with revelation of why God desires to bless His people. We are told in this passage that His *"divine power has given to us all things that pertain to life."* In other words, God has already made provision for every area of life. There is not a single area in your life where God does not desire to bless and have His influence for good. There are promises and rewards that cover every aspect of your life, either directly or in principle.

God has already made provision for every area and need in your life.

Also, note the phrase *"through these you may be partakers of the divine nature."* Peter is showing us that when we partake of God's promises, we are really experiencing God Himself. For example, when we experience God's promise of peace or joy, we are actually experiencing God's peace and joy within Himself. When we experience God's supernatural provision, we are experiencing a part and measure of Heaven here on earth. This is why Jesus said when we pray we are to say,

> Your Kingdom come, Your will be done… Matthew 6:10

Jesus is telling us to ask for His rewards on this earth. He is encouraging us to receive Heaven on earth now. When we pray "Kingdom come" we are releasing the provision of God on this earth today.

The Reward for Living the Inspired Life

We are wrapping up this book with a chapter on God's rewards because living the inspired life is really a life of living out God's rewards and provisions. We started off this book by stating that the inspired life is all about knowing Jesus Christ and as a result, experiencing His *zoe* life.

You know Jesus when you experience Him. When you experience Him, you realize He desires to fill you and bless you with His presence and promises. So, we have come full circle.

Knowing Jesus Christ brings His life into yours. And His life in yours is experienced as He rewards you with all that He is. Truly you can live an inspired life because the originator of life is alive in you now, today. Friends, Jesus Christ wants you to know Him and to experience all that He is. He gave His life on a cross as your substitute so that you can be brought back into a relationship with Him.

When you receive the promises of God, it's as if the Master reaches down and touches your life with His life. God is giving of Himself to you. And as you open your heart, follow Jesus, and walk with Him, you will be elevated into a new realm of living.

Yes, you will live the inspired life giving, blessing, overcoming, growing, and walking this earth with the same potential as Jesus when He walked some 2000 years ago.

When you receive the promises of God, it's as if the Master reaches down and touches your life with His life.

There is an invitation from Heaven to you today to know Jesus Christ and live the life style He lived while He was on this earth. There is a call today for God to show Himself strong on your behalf. Eternity is stamped in your heart and the Holy Spirit is yearning to come alive in you. So today, decide to place yourself in a position to be rewarded. Walk with God and you will be blessed. Know Jesus Christ and you have before you the opportunity of a lifetime.

Epilogue

Jesus Christ was, and still is, the most inspired life to have ever graced this earth. His work and presence is continuing to impact and radically influence everyone's lives. Regardless of where a person is physically or culturally, God is making sure everyone hears and everyone has an opportunity to meet this God-Man who lived among us, died on the cross for us, and is still empowering His people to live an inspired life as He did.

It will go down in history that the most inspiring, powerful, and influential people were those who received Jesus Christ as their Lord and allowed Him to fill their lives with His presence and anointing. You, too, can decide today to join the ranks of believers throughout the world who rise up to live an inspired life.

Today you have a choice to know Jesus Christ in a vibrant, real, and personal way. You have a choice today to follow Him and become one of His disciples. We encourage you to make the choice to get connected to His plan, His people, and His church and in so doing, team up to influence the very community in which you live.

Friends, you have the opportunity to be filled with His Spirit and live within the realm of His Kingdom. You can bring Heaven to earth wherever you live, walk, and work. You can pray, speak to the mountains of despair and bondage, and overcome life's challenges. You can give away what God has done for you and literally change the course of history in someone else's life.

Our prayer for those who read this book is that the presence of the Holy Spirit will envelop and quicken you to rise to a new level of living. Yes, rise up and take a stand as a person who will be inspired and inspire others for God.

Our prayer is that you not only read this book, but also make a decision to live out the principles of this book. Take the time to meditate and pray through again what you have read. Get out a highlighter and mark up this book. Underline the scriptures which come alive in your life. Take action and join others who decide to live an inspired life.

This is our prayer for you. And when everything is over, and the days on earth come to an end, we'll see you on the other side, standing with the millions who have gone before and those, too, who have lived out "The Inspired Life—God's Dream for Your Life."

Notes

Notes

Notes

Notes

Notes

Notes

Notes

Notes

Notes

Notes

www.ingramcontent.com/pod-product-compliance
Lightning Source LLC
Chambersburg PA
CBHW070810100426
42742CB00012B/2317